NIST Special Publication 800-113

Guide to SSL VPNs

Recommendations of the National Institute of Standards and Technology

Sheila Frankel
Paul Hoffman
Angela Orebaugh
Richard Park

COMPUTER SECURITY

Computer Security Division
Information Technology Laboratory
National Institute of Standards and Technology
Gaithersburg, MD 20899-8930

July 2008

U.S. Department of Commerce

Carlos M. Gutierrez, Secretary

National Institute of Standards and Technology

James M. Turner, Deputy Director

Reports on Computer Systems Technology

The Information Technology Laboratory (ITL) at the National Institute of Standards and Technology (NIST) promotes the U.S. economy and public welfare by providing technical leadership for the nation's measurement and standards infrastructure. ITL develops tests, test methods, reference data, proof of concept implementations, and technical analysis to advance the development and productive use of information technology. ITL's responsibilities include the development of technical, physical, administrative, and management standards and guidelines for the cost-effective security and privacy of sensitive unclassified information in Federal computer systems. This Special Publication 800-series reports on ITL's research, guidance, and outreach efforts in computer security and its collaborative activities with industry, government, and academic organizations.

> Certain commercial entities, equipment, or materials may be identified in this document in order to describe an experimental procedure or concept adequately. Such identification is not intended to imply recommendation or endorsement by the National Institute of Standards and Technology, nor is it intended to imply that the entities, materials, or equipment are necessarily the best available for the purpose.

Acknowledgements

The authors, Sheila Frankel of the National Institute of Standards and Technology (NIST), Paul Hoffman of the Virtual Private Network Consortium (VPNC), and Angela Orebaugh and Richard Park of Booz Allen Hamilton, wish to thank their colleagues who reviewed drafts of this document and contributed to its technical content, especially Elaine Barker, Jim St. Pierre and Tim Polk of NIST. The authors would like to acknowledge Tim Grance and Karen Scarfone of NIST for their keen and insightful assistance throughout the development of the document. The authors particularly want to thank Guy Snyder, Darren Hartman and Thang Phan of ICSA Labs for their careful review and valuable contributions to improving the quality of this publication. The authors would also like to express their thanks to Mike Hillhouse of Juniper Networks and Mahesh Jethanandani of Cisco for their worthwhile comments and suggestions.

Table of Contents

Executive Summary **ES-1**

1. Introduction **1-1**
    1.1 Authority 1-1
    1.2 Purpose and Scope 1-1
    1.3 Audience 1-1
    1.4 Document Structure 1-1

2. Network and Transport Layer Security **2-1**
    2.1 The Need for Network and Transport Layer Security 2-1
    2.2 Virtual Private Networking (VPN) 2-4
        2.2.1 SSL Portal VPNs 2-5
        2.2.2 SSL Tunnel VPNs 2-5
        2.2.3 Administering SSL VPNs 2-5
    2.3 Summary 2-6

3. SSL VPN Fundamentals **3-1**
    3.1 SSL VPN Architecture 3-1
    3.2 SSL VPN Functions 3-2
    3.3 SSL VPN Features and Security Services 3-3
        3.3.1 Manageability 3-4
        3.3.2 High Availability and Scalability 3-4
        3.3.3 Portal Customization 3-5
        3.3.4 Authentication 3-5
        3.3.5 Encryption and Integrity Protection 3-6
        3.3.6 Access Control 3-6
        3.3.7 Endpoint Security Controls 3-8
        3.3.8 Intrusion Prevention 3-9
    3.4 SSL Protocol Basics 3-9
        3.4.1 Versions of SSL and TLS 3-9
        3.4.2 Cryptography Used in SSL Sessions 3-10
        3.4.3 Authentication Used for Identifying SSL Servers 3-10
    3.5 SSL VPN Challenges 3-11
    3.6 Summary 3-12

4. SSL VPN Planning and Implementation **4-1**
    4.1 Identify Requirements 4-1
    4.2 SSL VPNs and FIPS 140-2 Approval 4-2
        4.2.1 Versions of SSL 4-3
        4.2.2 Key Establishment Used by SSL 4-3
        4.2.3 Hash Functions Used by SSL 4-4
        4.2.4 SSL Encryption 4-4
        4.2.5 Certificates Used During SSL Negotiations 4-4
    4.3 Design the Solution 4-5
        4.3.1 Design the Access Control Policy 4-6
        4.3.2 Design the Endpoint Security Policy 4-9
        4.3.3 Select the Authentication Methods 4-11
        4.3.4 Design the Architecture 4-12

		4.3.5	Cryptography Policy and FIPS Compliance	4-23
		4.3.6	Other Design Decisions	4-23
		4.3.7	Summary of Design Decisions	4-24
	4.4	Implement and Test Prototype		4-25
		4.4.1	Application and Client Interoperability	4-27
	4.5	Deploy the Solution		4-28
	4.6	Manage the Solution		4-29
	4.7	Summary		4-30

5. **SSL VPN Recommended Practices** 5-1

6. **Alternatives to SSL VPNs** 6-1

    6.1 Data Link Layer VPN Protocols 6-1
    6.2 Network Layer VPN Protocols 6-2
    6.3 Application Layer "VPNs" 6-3
    6.4 Summary 6-3

7. **Case Study** 7-1

    7.1 Identifying Needs and Evaluating Options 7-1
    7.2 Designing the Solution 7-2
        7.2.1 Access Control Policy 7-2
        7.2.2 Endpoint Security Policy 7-3
        7.2.3 Authentication Scheme 7-4
        7.2.4 Architecture Design 7-4
        7.2.5 Selection of Hardware Configuration 7-4
        7.2.6 Device Placement and Firewall Configuration 7-5
        7.2.7 Routing Policy 7-5
        7.2.8 High Availability 7-5
        7.2.9 Management 7-5
        7.2.10 Client Software Selection 7-6
        7.2.11 Portal Design 7-6
        7.2.12 Encryption Scheme 7-6
    7.3 Implementing a Prototype 7-6
        7.3.1 Example configuration steps 7-6
    7.4 Deploying and Managing the Solution 7-8
    7.5 Summary 7-8

List of Appendices

Appendix A— Glossary A-1

Appendix B— Acronyms B-1

List of Figures

Figure 2-1. TCP/IP Layers 2-1
Figure 3-1. SSL VPN Architecture 3-2
Figure 4-1. Firewall with SSL VPN Functionality 4-14
Figure 4-2. SSL VPN Device in Internal Network 4-15
Figure 4-3. SSL VPN Device in DMZ Network 4-16
Figure 4-4. SSL VPN Device with Two Interfaces 4-17
Figure 4-5. Routing Problem with SSL VPN Traffic 4-20
Figure 4-6. Example Portal Interface 4-23

List of Tables

Table 3-1. Access Control Examples 3-7
Table 3-2. Access Control Examples with Endpoint Security Controls 3-8
Table 4-1. Sample Access Control Policy 4-9
Table 4-2. Sample Authentication Methods Table 4-12
Table 4-3. Design Decisions Checklist 4-24
Table 5-1. SSL VPN Life Cycle Phase Recommendations 5-1
Table 6-1. Comparison of SSL and Alternatives 6-4
Table 6-2. IP Protocols and TCP/UDP Port Numbers for VPN Protocols 6-5
Table 7-1. Organization's Access Control Policy 7-3
Table 7-2. Organization's Authentication Methods 7-4

Executive Summary

Secure Sockets Layer (SSL) virtual private networks (VPN) provide secure remote access to an organization's resources. A VPN is a virtual network, built on top of existing physical networks, that can provide a secure communications mechanism for data and other information transmitted between two endpoints. Because a VPN can be used over existing networks such as the Internet, it can facilitate the secure transfer of sensitive data across public networks. An SSL VPN consists of one or more VPN devices to which users connect using their Web browsers. The traffic between the Web browser and the SSL VPN device is encrypted with the SSL protocol or its successor, the Transport Layer Security (TLS) protocol. This type of VPN may be referred to as either an SSL VPN or a TLS VPN. This guide uses the term SSL VPN. SSL VPNs provide remote users with access to Web applications and client/server applications, and connectivity to internal networks. Despite the popularity of SSL VPNs, they are not intended to replace Internet Protocol Security (IPsec) VPNs.[1] The two VPN technologies are complementary and address separate network architectures and business needs. SSL VPNs offer versatility and ease of use because they use the SSL protocol, which is included with all standard Web browsers, so the client usually does not require configuration by the user. SSL VPNs offer granular control for a range of users on a variety of computers, accessing resources from many locations. There are two primary types of SSL VPNs:

- **SSL Portal VPNs.** This type of SSL VPN allows a user to use a single standard SSL connection to a Web site to securely access multiple network services. The site accessed is typically called a portal because it is a single page that leads to many other resources. The remote user accesses the SSL VPN gateway using any modern Web browser, identifies himself or herself to the gateway using an authentication method supported by the gateway, and is then presented with a Web page that acts as the portal to the other services.

- **SSL Tunnel VPNs.** This type of SSL VPN allows a user to use a typical Web browser to securely access multiple network services, including applications and protocols that are not web-based, through a tunnel that is running under SSL. SSL tunnel VPNs require that the Web browser be able to handle active content, which allows them to provide functionality that is not accessible to SSL portal VPNs. Examples of active content include Java, JavaScript, Active X, or Flash applications or plug-ins.

This publication discusses the fundamental technologies and features of SSL VPNs. It describes SSL and how it fits within the context of layered network security. It presents a phased approach to SSL VPN planning and implementation that can help in achieving successful SSL VPN deployments. It also compares the SSL VPN technology with IPsec VPNs and other VPN solutions. This information is particularly valuable for helping organizations to determine how best to deploy SSL VPNs within their specific network environments.

Implementing the following recommendations should assist in facilitating more efficient and effective SSL VPN use for Federal departments and agencies.

Federal agencies deploying SSL VPNs must configure them to only allow FIPS-compliant cryptographic algorithms, cipher suites, and versions of SSL.

Some organizations, such as Federal agencies, have strict requirements for encryption and integrity protection. SSL VPNs should support the required algorithms for symmetric encryption, key exchange, and hash functions. For government agencies, traffic that requires protection must employ Federal

---

[1] Detailed information on the IPsec components may be found in NIST Special Publication (SP) 800-77, *Guide to IPsec VPNs*, available from http://csrc.nist.gov/publications/nistpubs/.

Information Processing Standard (FIPS)-compliant cryptographic algorithms and modules. Many of the cryptographic algorithms used in some SSL cipher suites are not FIPS-approved, and therefore are not allowed for use in SSL VPNs that are to be used in applications that must conform to FIPS 140-2. This means that to be run in FIPS-compliant mode, an SSL VPN gateway must only allow cipher suites that are allowed by FIPS 140-2.

Some of the cryptographic requirements, including allowable hash functions and certificate key lengths, will change at the end of 2010. Therefore, Federal agencies who want to provide SSL VPN services after 2010 must ensure that their systems are upgradeable to the new FIPS-compliant cipher suites and key lengths before the end of 2010, and that their SSL VPN vendors guarantee that such upgrades will be available early enough for testing and deployment in the field.

Organizations planning SSL VPN deployments should identify and define requirements, and evaluate several products to determine their fit into the organization.

SSL VPN products vary in functionality, including protocol and application support. They also vary in breadth, depth, and completeness of features and security services. Some recommendations and considerations include the following:

- SSL VPN manageability features such as status reporting, logging, and auditing should provide adequate capabilities for the organization to effectively operate and manage the SSL VPN and to extract detailed usage information.

- The SSL VPN high availability and scalability features should support the organization's requirements for failover, load balancing and throughput. State and information sharing is recommended to keep the failover process transparent to the user.

- SSL VPN portal customization should allow the organization to control the look and feel of the portal and to customize the portal to support various devices such as personal digital assistants (PDA) and smart phones.

- SSL VPN authentication should provide the necessary support for the organization's current and future authentication methods and leverage existing authentication databases. SSL VPN authentication should also be tested to ensure interoperability with existing authentication methods.

- The strongest possible cryptographic algorithms and key lengths that are considered secure for current practice should be used for encryption and integrity protection unless they are incompatible with interoperability, performance and export constraints.

- SSL VPNs should be evaluated to ensure they provide the level of granularity needed for access controls. Access controls should be capable of applying permissions to users, groups, and resources, as well as integrating with endpoint security controls.

- Implementation of endpoint security controls is often the most diverse service amongst SSL VPN products. Endpoint security should be evaluated to ensure it provides the necessary host integrity checking and security protection mechanisms required for the organization.

- Not all SSL VPNs have integrated intrusion prevention capabilities. Those that do should be evaluated to ensure they do not introduce an unacceptable amount of latency into the network traffic.

Organizations should use a phased approach to SSL VPN planning and implementation.

A successful SSL VPN deployment can be achieved by following a clear, step-by-step planning and implementation process. The use of a phased approach can minimize unforeseen issues and identify potential pitfalls early in the process. The five phases of the recommended approach are as follows:

1. **Identify Requirements.** Identify the requirements for remote access and determine how they can best be met.

2. **Design the Solution.** Make design decisions in five areas: access control, endpoint security, authentication methods, architecture, and cryptography policy.

3. **Implement and Test a Prototype.** Test a prototype of the designed solution in a laboratory, test, or production environment to identify any potential issues.

4. **Deploy the Solution.** Gradually deploy the SSL VPN solution throughout the enterprise, beginning with a pilot program.

5. **Manage the Solution.** Maintain the SSL VPN components and resolve operational issues. Repeat the planning and implementation process when significant changes need to be incorporated into the solution.

Organizations should be familiar with the limitations of SSL VPN technology.

SSL VPNs, although a maturing technology, continue to face several challenges. These include limitations on their ability to support a large number of applications and clients, the methods of implementing network extension and endpoint security, the ability to provide clientless access, the use of the SSL VPN from public locations, and product and technology education.

Organizations should implement other measures that support and complement SSL VPN implementations.

These measures help to ensure that the SSL VPN solution is implemented in an environment with the technical, management, and operational controls necessary to provide sufficient security for the SSL VPN implementation. Examples of supporting measures include:

- Establishing and maintaining control over all entry and exit points for the protected network, which helps to ensure its integrity

- Incorporating SSL VPN considerations into organizational policies (e.g., identity management, remote access)

- Ensuring that all SSL VPN endpoints are secured and maintained properly to reduce the risk of SSL VPN compromise or misuse.

Although SSL VPNs are flexible enough to meet many needs, there are certain cases when other types of VPNs may provide a better solution. Network layer VPN protocols, primarily IPsec; data link layer VPN protocols, such as Point-to-Point Tunneling Protocol (PPTP), Layer 2 Tunneling Protocol (L2TP), and Layer 2 Forwarding (L2F); and application layer security protocols, including OpenPGP and Secure Shell (SSH), are all effective alternatives to SSL VPNs for particular needs and environments.

1. Introduction

1.1 Authority

The National Institute of Standards and Technology (NIST) developed this document in furtherance of its statutory responsibilities under the Federal Information Security Management Act (FISMA) of 2002, Public Law 107-347.

NIST is responsible for developing standards and guidelines, including minimum requirements, for providing adequate information security for all agency operations and assets; but such standards and guidelines shall not apply to national security systems. This guideline is consistent with the requirements of the Office of Management and Budget (OMB) Circular A-130, Section 8b(3), "Securing Agency Information Systems," as analyzed in A-130, Appendix IV: Analysis of Key Sections. Supplemental information is provided in A-130, Appendix III.

This guideline has been prepared for use by Federal agencies. It may be used by nongovernmental organizations on a voluntary basis and is not subject to copyright, though attribution is desired.

Nothing in this document should be taken to contradict standards and guidelines made mandatory and binding on Federal agencies by the Secretary of Commerce under statutory authority, nor should these guidelines be interpreted as altering or superseding the existing authorities of the Secretary of Commerce, Director of the OMB, or any other Federal official.

1.2 Purpose and Scope

This publication seeks to assist organizations in understanding SSL VPN technologies and in designing, implementing, configuring, securing, monitoring, and maintaining SSL VPN solutions. This document provides a phased approach to SSL VPN planning and implementation that can help in achieving successful SSL VPN deployments. It also provides a comparison with other similar technologies such as IPsec VPNs and other VPN solutions.

1.3 Audience

The publication has been created for computer security staff and program managers; system, network, and application administrators; and others who are considering the deployment of SSL VPNs. It is also useful for organizations that already deploy IPsec VPNs and want to know how IPsec and SSL VPNs are complementary.

1.4 Document Structure

The remainder of this document is organized into the following six major sections:

- Section 2 provides a general introduction to network and transport layer security.

- Section 3 gives describes the fundamentals of SSL VPNs and their services and features.

- Section 4 explores in depth each of the SSL VPN planning and implementation phases.

- Section 5 provides a consolidated list of recommended practices for SSL VPN deployment in terms of the system development life cycle approach.

- Section 6 describes several VPN protocols that are used as alternatives to SSL VPNs in different scenarios.

- Section 7 presents an SSL VPN solution planning and implementation case study.

The document also contains appendices with supporting material. Appendices A and B contain a glossary and an acronym list, respectively.

2. Network and Transport Layer Security

This section provides a general introduction to network and transport layer security. *Network layer security* protects network communications at the layer that is responsible for routing packets across networks. *Transport layer security* provides security at the layer responsible for end-to-end communications. This section first introduces the Transmission Control Protocol/Internet Protocol (TCP/IP) model and its layers and then discusses the need to use security controls at each layer to protect communications. It provides a brief introduction to Secure Sockets Layer (SSL) and its successor, Transport Layer Security (TLS), primarily focused on the types of protection that SSL can provide for communications. This section also provides a brief introduction to virtual private networking (VPN) services and explains what types of protection a VPN can provide. It introduces three VPN architecture models and discusses the features and common uses of each model. This document discusses only the most common VPN scenarios and uses of SSL.

2.1 The Need for Network and Transport Layer Security

TCP/IP is widely used throughout the world to provide network communications. TCP/IP communications are composed of four layers that work together. When a user wants to transfer data across networks, the data is passed from the highest layer through intermediate layers to the lowest layer, with each layer adding information. At each layer, the logical units are typically composed of a header and a payload. The *payload* consists of the information passed down from the previous layer, while the *header* contains layer-specific information such as addresses. At the application layer, the payload is the actual application data. The lowest layer sends the accumulated data through the physical network; the data is then passed up through the layers to its destination. Essentially, the data produced by a layer is encapsulated in a larger container by the layer below it. The four TCP/IP layers, from highest to lowest, are shown in Figure 2-1.

Application Layer. This layer sends and receives data for particular applications, such as Domain Name System (DNS), HyperText Transfer Protocol (HTTP), and Simple Mail Transfer Protocol (SMTP).
Transport Layer. This layer provides connection-oriented or connectionless services for transporting application layer services between networks. The transport layer can optionally assure the reliability of communications. Transmission Control Protocol (TCP) and User Datagram Protocol (UDP) are commonly used transport layer protocols.
Network Layer. This layer routes packets across networks. Internet Protocol (IP) is the fundamental network layer protocol for TCP/IP. Other commonly used protocols at the network layer are Internet Control Message Protocol (ICMP) and Internet Group Management Protocol (IGMP).
Data Link Layer. This layer handles communications on the physical network components. The best-known data link layer protocol is Ethernet.

Figure 2-1. TCP/IP Layers

Security controls exist for network communications at each layer of the TCP/IP model. As previously explained, data is passed from the highest to the lowest layer, with each layer adding more information. Because of this, a security control at a higher layer cannot provide protection for lower layers, because the lower layers perform functions of which the higher layers are not aware. Security controls that are available at each layer include:

- **Application Layer.** Separate controls must be established for each application. For example, if an application needs to protect sensitive data sent across networks, the application may need to be modified to provide this protection. While this provides a very high degree of control and flexibility over the application's security, it may require a large resource investment to add and configure controls properly for each application. Designing a cryptographically sound application protocol is very difficult, and implementing it properly is even more challenging, so creating new application layer security controls is likely to create vulnerabilities. Also, some applications, particularly off-the-shelf software, may not be capable of providing such protection. While application layer controls can protect application data, they cannot protect TCP/IP information such as IP addresses because this information exists at a lower layer. Whenever possible, application layer controls for protecting network communications should be standards-based solutions that have been in use for some time. One example is Secure Multipurpose Internet Mail Extensions (S/MIME), which is commonly used to encrypt email messages.[2]

- **Transport Layer.** Controls at this layer can be used to protect the data in a single communication session between two hosts. Because IP information is added at the network layer, transport layer controls cannot protect it. The most common use for transport layer protocols is securing HTTP traffic; the Transport Layer Security (TLS)[3] protocol is usually used for this. The use of TLS typically requires each application to support TLS; however, unlike application layer controls, which typically involve extensive customization of the application, transport layer controls such as TLS are much less intrusive because they do not need to understand the application's functions or characteristics. Although using TLS may require modifying some applications, TLS is a well-tested protocol that has several implementations that have been added to many applications, so it is a relatively low-risk option compared to adding protection at the application layer. Traditionally TLS has been used to protect HTTP-based communications and can be used with SSL portal VPNs.

- **Network Layer.** Controls at this layer can be applied to all applications; thus, they are not application-specific. For example, all network communications between two hosts or networks can be protected at this layer without modifying any applications on the clients or the servers. In some environments, network layer controls such as Internet Protocol Security (IPsec) provide a much better solution than transport or application layer controls because of the difficulties in adding controls to individual applications. Network layer controls also provide a way for network administrators to enforce certain security policies. Another advantage of network layer controls is that since IP information (e.g., IP addresses) is added at this layer, the controls can protect both the data within the packets and the IP information for each packet. However, network layer controls provide less control and flexibility for protecting specific applications than transport and application layer controls. SSL tunnel VPNs provide the ability to secure both TCP and UDP communications including client/server and other network traffic, and therefore act as network layer VPNs.

- **Data Link Layer.** Data link layer controls are applied to all communications on a specific physical link, such as a dedicated circuit between two buildings or a dial-up modem connection to an Internet Service Provider (ISP). Data link layer controls for dedicated circuits are most often provided by specialized hardware devices known as *data link encryptors*; data link layer controls for other types of connections, such as dial-up modem communications, are usually provided through software. Because the data link layer is below the network layer, controls at this layer can protect both data and IP information. Compared to controls at the other layers, data link layer controls are relatively simple, which makes them easier to implement; also, they support other network layer protocols besides IP. Because data link layer controls are specific to a particular physical link, they cannot

---

[2] Several Request for Comment (RFC) documents from the Internet Engineering Task Force (IETF) define S/MIME, as well as standards for using it to protect email messages. One example is RFC 3852, *Cryptographic Message Syntax (CMS)*, available at http://www.ietf.org/rfc/rfc3852.txt.

[3] TLS is the standards-based version of SSL version 3. More information on TLS is available in RFC 4346, *The TLS Protocol Version 1.1*, available at http://www.ietf.org/rfc/rfc4346.txt. Another good source of information is NIST SP 800-52, *Guidelines on the Selection and Use of Transport Layer Security*, available from http://csrc.nist.gov/publications/nistpubs/.

protect connections with multiple links, such as establishing a VPN over the Internet. An Internet-based connection is typically composed of several physical links chained together; protecting such a connection with data link layer controls would require deploying a separate control to each link, which is not feasible. Data link layer protocols have been used for many years primarily to provide additional protection for specific physical links that should not be trusted.

Because they can provide protection for many applications at once without modifying them, network layer security controls have been used frequently for securing communications, particularly over shared networks such as the Internet. Network layer security controls provide a single solution for protecting data from all applications, as well as protecting IP information. Nevertheless, in many cases, controls at another layer are better suited to providing protection than network layer controls. For example, if only one or two applications need protection, a network layer control may be excessive. Transport layer protocols such as SSL are most commonly used to provide security for communications with individual HTTP-based applications, although they are also used to provide protection for communication sessions of other types of applications such as SMTP, Point of Presence (POP), Internet Message Access Protocol (IMAP), and File Transfer Protocol (FTP). Because all major Web browsers include support for TLS, users who wish to use Web-based applications that are protected by TLS normally do not need to install any client software or reconfigure their systems. Newer applications of transport layer security protocols protect both HTTP and non-HTTP application communications, including client/server applications and other network traffic. Controls at each layer offer advantages and features that controls at other layers do not. Section 3 contains detailed information on transport layer security controls. Information on data link, network, and application layer alternatives to transport layer controls is provided in Section 6.

IPsec[4] has emerged as the most commonly used network layer security control for protecting communications, while SSL is the most commonly used transport layer security control. Depending on how IPsec and SSL are implemented and configured, both can provide any combination of the following types of protection:

- **Confidentiality.** IPsec and SSL can ensure that data cannot be read by unauthorized parties. This is accomplished by encrypting data using a cryptographic algorithm and a secret key—a value known only to the two parties exchanging data. The data can only be decrypted by someone who has the secret key.

- **Integrity.** IPsec and SSL can determine if data has been changed (intentionally or unintentionally) during transit. The integrity of data can be assured by generating a message authentication code (MAC) value, which is a keyed cryptographic checksum of the data. If the data is altered and the MAC is recalculated, the old and new MACs will differ.

- **Peer Authentication.** Each IPsec endpoint confirms the identity of the other IPsec endpoint with which it wishes to communicate, ensuring that the network traffic and data is being sent from the expected host. SSL authentication is typically performed one-way, authenticating the server to the client; however, SSL VPNs require authentication for both endpoints.

- **Replay Protection.** The same data is not delivered multiple times, and data is not delivered grossly out of order.

- **Traffic Analysis Protection.** A person monitoring network traffic cannot determine the contents of the network traffic or how much data is being exchanged. IPsec can also conceal which parties are communicating, whereas SSL leaves this information exposed. Frequency of communication may

---

[4] The IPsec protocols were developed within the IPsec Working Group of the IETF.

also be protected depending on implementation. Nevertheless, the number of packets being exchanged can be counted.

- **Access Control.** IPsec and SSL endpoints can perform filtering to ensure that only authorized users can access particular network resources. IPsec and SSL endpoints can also allow or block certain types of network traffic, such as allowing Web server access but denying file sharing.

2.2 Virtual Private Networking (VPN)

A *VPN* is a virtual network, built on top of existing physical networks, that can provide a secure communications mechanism for data and other information transmitted between networks. Because a VPN can be used over existing networks, such as the Internet, it can facilitate the secure transfer of sensitive data across public networks. This is often less expensive than alternatives such as dedicated private telecommunications lines between organizations or branch offices. VPNs can also provide flexible solutions, such as securing communications between remote telecommuters and the organization's servers, regardless of where the telecommuters are located. A VPN can even be established within a single network to protect particularly sensitive communications from other parties on the same network.

It is important to understand that VPNs do not remove all risk from networking. While VPNs can greatly reduce risk, particularly for communications that occur over public networks, they cannot eliminate all risk for such communications. One potential problem is the strength of the implementation. For example, flaws in an encryption algorithm or the software implementing the algorithm could allow attackers to decrypt intercepted traffic; random number generators that do not produce sufficiently random values could provide additional attack possibilities. Another issue is encryption key disclosure; an attacker who discovers a key could not only decrypt traffic but potentially also pose as a legitimate user. Another area of risk involves availability. A common model for information assurance is based on the concepts of confidentiality, integrity, and availability. Although VPNs are designed to support confidentiality and integrity, they generally do not improve *availability*, the ability for authorized users to access systems as needed. In fact, many VPN implementations actually tend to decrease availability somewhat, because they add more components and services to the existing network infrastructure. This is highly dependent upon the chosen VPN architecture model and the details of the implementation.

The following sections describe the two primary types of SSL VPNs: *SSL portal VPNs* and *SSL tunnel VPNs*. (There is a third type, SSL gateway-to-gateway VPNs, that is available in some implementations. These are rarely used because they have very similar features to IPsec VPNs but less flexibility; they are therefore not discussed in this document.) Both types of SSL VPNs are typically used to provide remote users access to multiple services controlled and administered by the SSL VPN gateway.

SSL VPN gateways are sometimes single-purpose hardware systems that contain the software needed to perform the SSL VPN tasks. In other cases, firewall and router hardware systems contain SSL VPN capabilities and thus become SSL VPN gateways when those capabilities are turned on in the system's administrative interface.

It should be noted that, although there are standards for the TLS protocol, there are currently no standards for any type of SSL VPN.[5] For example, SSL VPN features such as access control and endpoint security have not been standardized. Thus, the descriptions here are based on common implementations of SSL VPNs at the time this document was being prepared.

---

[5] The TLS protocol standards are described in RFC 4346, *The TLS Protocol Version 1.1*, available at http://www.ietf.org/rfc/rfc4346.txt.

2.2.1 SSL Portal VPNs

An SSL portal VPN allows a user to use a single standard SSL connection to a Web site to securely access multiple network services. The site accessed is typically called a *portal* because it has a single page that leads to many other resources. SSL portal VPNs act as transport-layer VPNs that work over a single network port, namely the TCP port for SSL-protected HTTP (443).

The remote user accesses the SSL VPN gateway using any modern Web browser, identifies himself or herself to the gateway using an authentication method supported by the gateway, and then is presented with a Web page that acts as the portal to the other services. These other services might be links to other Web servers, shared file directories, Web-based email systems, applications that run on protected servers, and any other services that can be channeled through a Web page.

To the user, an SSL portal VPN is a Web site with more options of services available after the user has authenticated. To access an SSL portal VPN, the user enters the portal's URL in a Web browser just as the user would enter the URL for any other Web page. These URLs typically use the https: scheme to start SSL immediately, but many SSL VPNs allow users to first enter an http: URL that then redirects to a secure SSL port.

SSL portal VPNs work with essentially any modern Web browser. Specifically, they work with browsers whether or not the browsers allow (or support) active content. Thus, SSL portal VPNs are accessible to more users than SSL tunnel VPNs.

2.2.2 SSL Tunnel VPNs

An SSL tunnel VPN allows a user to use a typical Web browser to securely access multiple network services through a tunnel that is running under SSL. SSL tunnel VPNs require that the Web browser be able to handle specific types of active content (e.g., Java, JavaScript, Flash, or ActiveX) and that the user be able to run them. (Most browsers that handle such applications and plug-ins also allow the user or administrator to block them from being executed.)

The "tunnel" in an SSL tunnel VPN is both similar and quite different from the tunnels seen in typical IPsec VPNs. The two types of tunnels are similar in that almost all IP traffic is fully protected by the tunnel, giving the user full access to services on the network protected by the VPN gateway. The tunnels are quite different in that SSL/VPN tunnels are usually created in SSL using a non-standard tunneling method, while IPsec tunnels are created with methods described in the IPsec standard.

The tunneling in an SSL tunnel VPN allows a wide variety of protocols and applications to be run through it. For example, essentially any protocol that runs over TCP or UDP can be tunneled through such a gateway, making the remote user's experience of the protected network very similar to being directly on the network. To the user, an SSL tunnel VPN may appear quite different from a typical Web site because the tunneling plug-in or application needs to be loaded into the user's browser before the user can access the VPN. This might involve warning messages about the software being loaded, and it could also prevent users from entering the VPN if their Web browsers are instructed not to allow such programs to run. Because of the active content requirement, SSL tunnel VPNs may be accessible to fewer users than SSL portal VPNs.

2.2.3 Administering SSL VPNs

The administration of both SSL portal VPNs and SSL tunnel VPNs is similar. The gateway administrator needs to specify local policy in at least two broad areas:

- **Access**. All SSL VPNs allow the administrator to specify which users have access to the VPN services. User authentication might be done with a simple password through a Web form, or through more sophisticated authentication mechanisms.

- **Capabilities**. The administrator can specify the services to which each authorized user has access. For example, some users might have access to only certain Web pages, while others might have access to those Web pages plus other services.

Different SSL VPNs have very different administrative interfaces and very different capabilities for allowing access and specifying allowed actions for users. For example, many but not all SSL VPNs allow validation of users through the Remote Authentication Dial-In User Server (RADIUS) protocol. As another example, some SSL VPNs allow the administrator to create groups of users who have the same access methods and capabilities; this makes adding new users to the system easier than gateways that require the administrator to specify both of these for each new user.

2.3 Summary

Section 2 describes the TCP/IP model and its layers—application, transport, network, and data link—and explained how security controls at each layer provide different types of protection for TCP/IP communications. SSL, a transport layer security control, can provide several types of protection for data, depending on its configuration. The section describes SSL VPNs and highlights the two primary SSL VPN architecture models (SSL portal VPNs and SSL tunnel VPNs). The following summarizes the key points from Section 2:

- TCP/IP is widely used throughout the world to provide network communications. The TCP/IP model is composed of the following four layers, each having its own security controls that provide different types of protection:

    - **Application layer**, which sends and receives data for particular applications. Separate controls must be established for each application; this provides a very high degree of control and flexibility over each application's security, but it may be very resource-intensive. However, inventing new application layer security controls can create vulnerabilities. Another potential issue is that some applications may not be capable of providing such protection or of being modified to do so.

    - **Transport layer**, which provides connection-oriented or connectionless services for transporting application layer services across networks. Controls at this layer can protect the data in a single communications session between two hosts. The most frequently used transport layer control is SSL, which most often secures HTTP traffic but is also used to implement VPNs. To be used, transport layer controls must be supported by both the clients and servers. SSL portal VPNs operate at the transport layer.

    - **Network layer**, which routes packets across networks. Controls at this layer apply to all applications and are not application-specific, so applications do not have to be modified to use the controls. However, network layer controls provide less control and flexibility for protecting specific applications than transport and application layer controls. Network layer controls can protect both the data within packets and the IP information for each packet. IPsec VPNs operate at the network layer; since they can secure both TCP and UDP traffic, SSL tunnel VPNs operate as network layer VPNs.

    - **Data link layer**, which handles communications on the physical network components. Data link layer controls are suitable for protecting a specific physical link, such as a dedicated circuit between two buildings or a dial-up modem connection to an ISP. Because each physical link must be secured separately, data link layer controls generally are not feasible for protecting connections that involve several links, such as connections across the Internet.

- IPsec is a framework of open standards for ensuring private communications over IP networks which has become the most commonly used network layer security control. SSL is an open standards track protocol that provides secure communications at the transport layer. Both protocols can provide several types of protection, including maintaining confidentiality and integrity, authenticating the origin of data, preventing packet replay and traffic analysis, and providing access protection.

- A VPN is a virtual network built on top of existing networks that can provide a secure communications mechanism for data and IP information transmitted between networks.

- Although VPNs can reduce the risks of networking, they cannot eliminate it. For example, a VPN implementation may have flaws in algorithms or software that attackers can exploit. Also, VPN implementations often have at least a slight negative impact on availability, because they add components and services to existing network infrastructures.

- There are two primary models for SSL VPN architectures:

    - **SSL portal VPN**. These VPNs allow remote users with almost any Web browser to connect to a VPN gateway and access services from a Web site provided on the gateway. SSL portal VPNs are more accessible to a wider range of users than SSL tunnel VPNs because they can be run on more Web browsers, particularly those whose security policies prevent running of active content that is downloaded from the Internet.

    - **SSL tunnel VPN**. These VPNs allow remote users with Web browsers that allow active content to access the network protected by a VPN gateway. SSL tunnel VPNs have many more capabilities than SSL portal VPNs because more services can be provided more easily.

3. SSL VPN Fundamentals

SSL VPNs provide secure remote access to an organization's resources. An SSL VPN consists of one or more VPN devices that users connect to using their Web browsers. The traffic between the Web browser and SSL VPN device is encrypted with the SSL protocol. SSL VPNs provide remote users with access to Web applications and client/server applications, and with connectivity to internal networks. They offer versatility and ease of use because they use the SSL protocol that is included with all standard Web browsers, so the client usually does not require configuration by the user.

This section of the document discusses SSL VPNs and their services and features. Section 3.1 provides an overview of the high-level SSL VPN architecture. Section 3.2 highlights the major functions of an SSL VPN. Section 3.3 describes the various features and services provided by SSL VPNs and the security controls used to protect the confidentiality, integrity, and availability of data. Section 3.4 briefly covers the technical details of the SSL and TLS protocols. Section 3.5 addresses the challenges involved with SSL VPNs.

3.1 SSL VPN Architecture

Figure 3-1 provides a high level view of a typical SSL VPN architecture. That architecture is the same for both SSL portal VPNs and SSL tunnel VPNs.

Typical SSL VPN users include people in remote offices, mobile users, business partners, and customers. Hardware clients include various types of devices, such as public kiosks, home personal computers (PC), PDAs, or smart phones, which may or may not be controlled or managed by the organization. The SSL VPN may also be accessed from any location including an airport, a coffee shop, or a hotel room, as long as the location has connectivity to the Internet and the user has a Web client that is capable of using the particular SSL VPN. All traffic is encrypted as it traverses public networks such as the Internet. The SSL VPN gateway is the endpoint for the secure connection and provides various services and features (most SSL VPN products are standalone hardware appliances, although there are some software-based solutions that are installed on user-supplied servers).

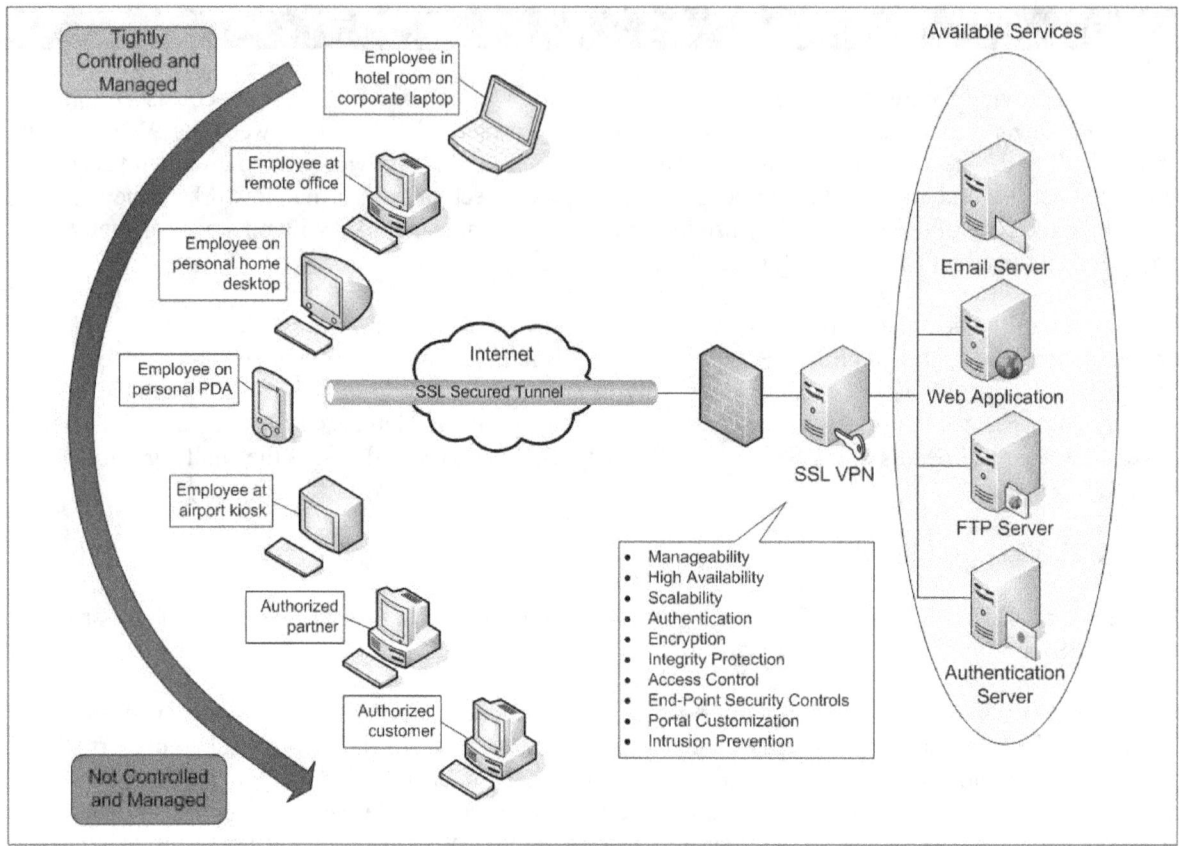

Figure 3-1. SSL VPN Architecture

3.2 SSL VPN Functions

Providing secure remote access to a wide variety of users and devices at many locations calls for a diverse set of SSL VPN services and features. Most SSL VPNs have one or more of the following three core functions:

- **Proxying.** A *proxy* is an intermediary device or program that provides communication and other services between a client and server. It has the ability to represent itself as the server to the client, and vice versa. A proxy may service requests internally or translate the information and pass it on to other servers. Proxying is a core function of an SSL portal VPN. The simplest form of an SSL portal VPN involves secure proxying of Web pages. The SSL portal VPN acts as a gateway by mediating the traffic between the user and the application. It receives the request from the user, connects to the Web server, downloads the information, and sends the information back to the user over the SSL connection. The proxy performs encryption or decryption and content inspection on each packet, which causes slightly slower performance.

- **Application Translation.** *Application translation* converts information from one protocol to another. It is often used to convert a legacy or proprietary protocol into a more widely used or standard protocol. It is also used to facilitate system integration and communication between applications and devices. Application translation uses proxying to interact with both sides of the connection with the appropriate protocol. SSL portal VPNs use application translation for applications that are not Web-enabled. This allows users to use a Web browser to access applications that do not have their own Web interfaces. For example, to provide file server access, an SSL portal

VPN would communicate with a file server using the appropriate protocol, such as the Common Internet File System (CIFS) or the File Transfer Protocol (FTP), and translate the information into a Web-based format so that users can view the information with a Web browser. Application translation requires a translator engine for each protocol that is supported.

- **Network Extension.** *Network extension* is a method of providing partial or complete network access to remote users. Users can connect to the network and access internal resources as if they were physically located on the internal local area network (LAN). This eliminates the need for creating Web-specific portals for all applications that require remote access. An SSL tunnel VPN network extension provides a secure connection from the user's system to an organization's network. This host-to-gateway tunnel can handle arbitrary traffic, much like a host-to-gateway IPsec VPN can. SSL tunnel VPN devices can support full or split tunneling. *Full tunneling* causes all network traffic to go through the tunnel to the organization. *Split tunneling* routes organization-specific traffic through the SSL VPN tunnel, but other traffic uses the remote user's default gateway. Network extension requires a client to be installed either as a plug-in in the user's Web browser or as a program on the user's system, which in turn requires administrative access to the local system. The client is typically an active content agent, so the system must have the ability to load the agent and the necessary privileges to run it. This can cause challenges on public systems, where users might not have those privileges, and on managed systems where security policy prevents such applets and controls. A more limited form of network extension is sometimes called *port forwarding*.

The three core functions allow SSL VPNs to provide secure remote access to a variety of applications. SSL VPN products vary in quality and effectiveness by the way they implement these three core functions. For example, SSL VPN products may offer support for different protocols via proxy and application translation; others might offer more or less control of the level of network access for network extensions. When evaluating SSL VPN products, it is important to have identified the remote access needs and applications served.

3.3 SSL VPN Features and Security Services

In addition to the three core functions, SSL VPNs include other features and security services. These elements often vary in breadth, depth, and completeness, so side-by-side comparisons of SSL VPN products often result in more differences than similarities. Therefore, it is important to identify and define requirements, and evaluate several products. Common SSL VPN features include the following:

- **Manageability**. Manageability includes device management, status reporting, logging, and auditing.
- **High availability**. High availability is a failover feature to ensure availability during device or component interruptions.
- **Scalability**. Scalability is the ability to support more users, concurrent sessions, and throughput than a single SSL VPN device can typically handle. Scalability is often integrated with high availability by balancing the VPN load amongst multiple SSL VPN devices.
- **Customization**. Customization is the ability to control the appearance of the SSL VPN Web pages that the users see when they first access the VPN. Besides layout and color preferences, customized portals are often necessary to support PDAs and smart phones over the SSL VPN.

Common SSL VPN security services include the following:

- **Authentication**. Authentication is the process a VPN uses to limit access to protected services by forcing users to identify themselves. This feature includes the ability to support strong authentication and to integrate with current authentication mechanisms.

- **Encryption and integrity protection.** Encryption protects the confidentiality of data as it traverses the Internet, while integrity protection ensures that the data is not altered as it traverses the Internet. Both are inherent in SSL.

- **Access control.** Access control permits or restricts access to applications at a granular level, such as per-user, per-group, and per-resource.

- **Endpoint security controls.** Endpoint security controls validate the security compliance of the client system that is attempting to use the SSL VPN. For example, host integrity checks may verify that firewall, malware detection and antivirus software are enabled and running on the client system, and the host is up-to-date on its patches. Endpoint security controls also include security protection mechanisms, such as Web browser cache cleaners, that remove sensitive information from client systems.

- **Intrusion prevention.** Intrusion prevention involves inspecting the data after it has been decrypted in the SSL VPN for potential attacks. It may also include anti-malware functionality to detect viruses, worms, and other malicious payloads and block or change network access rights based on the results of such checks.

Sections 3.3.1 through 3.3.8 provide details and examples of the various SSL VPN features and security services.

3.3.1 Manageability

SSL VPNs offer a variety of manageability features such as status reporting, logging, and auditing. Status reporting includes identifying connected users and reporting usage data in a graphical format. Logging includes the ability to export logs, debug logging, and automate log rollover. Auditing includes auditing application access, RADIUS-based accounting, and persistent storage of auditing information. Another manageability feature is the ability to terminate sessions as needed.

A manageability feature that is often overlooked is documentation. It is beneficial to have documentation for SSL VPN usage, configuration, and troubleshooting. Documentation may also include context-sensitive help within the management interface.

Another manageability feature that is beneficial for SSL VPNs is partitioned or delegated management. This allows different aspects of the SSL VPN device to be managed by different groups or individuals. This feature can be beneficial for service providers, collocation facilities, and organizations with different groups sharing the SSL VPN device. It is also quite useful for an SSL VPN to be able to be managed remotely, such as by a system administrator who is not on-site. Remote management requires greater security to prevent attackers from watching and possibly altering the management sessions; in SSL VPNs, this security is normally provided by running all remote management sessions under SSL.

3.3.2 High Availability and Scalability

Two other important features for SSL VPNs are high availability and scalability. High availability solutions use two or more SSL VPN devices configured in either active/passive or active/active mode. In an *active/passive* solution, one device actively services connections, while the other device is waiting in standby mode. The two devices continuously exchange "heartbeat" messages to communicate their status with one another. If the standby device does not receive a heartbeat message from the active device for a preconfigured time period, it will assume that the active device is no longer operating and take over servicing connections. In an *active/active* solution, both devices are actively servicing connections at the same time. If one device fails, the other device will service all connections if it has been properly sized to do so. High availability allows the SSL VPN to survive the loss of a device or device component.

In either active/passive or active/active mode, one of the challenges of high availability is properly propagating and sharing information between the devices. Another challenge is maintaining state information about existing connections in the event of a failure. SSL VPN proxying and network extension functionality each handle state information differently. Another consideration is transparency of failover to the users. Depending on how state information is shared, the user may or may not need to re-authenticate after a failure.

SSL VPNs support scalability with load-balancing features. Both high availability and load balancing often use a virtual IP address that is shared across multiple SSL VPN devices. In an active/passive architecture, the passive device has the ability to take over the virtual IP address and associated traffic if the active device fails. In an active/active architecture, both devices service the virtual IP address. SSL VPN devices configured as active/passive typically are not providing any scalability features, whereas active/active configurations use either an integrated load balancer or an external load balancer to distribute connections across multiple VPN devices. However, for the VPN to maintain functionality when one of the devices fails, it is essential to ensure that the VPN traffic load does not exceed the throughput capability of a single device.

3.3.3 Portal Customization

Portal customization is a feature that allows an administrator to control the appearance of the SSL VPN Web interface that the end users see and with which they interact. Note that both SSL portal VPNs and SSL tunnel VPNs usually have portal pages: SSL tunnel VPNs often have portal pages for users to change their settings, request help from a system administrator, and so on.

Some products lack portal customization features; nevertheless, finding the right files on the SSL VPN device and editing them may allow customization of the look and feel of the portal. Other products have built-in configuration settings to control the colors, icons, and layout of the portal. Some products only provide system-wide customization, while others allow portal customization on a per-group basis. Besides layout and color preferences, customized portals are often necessary to support PDAs and smart phones over SSL VPNs. Some products allow portal customization per system type to accommodate the limited functionality of PDAs and smart phones. Portal customization sometimes integrates with the endpoint security controls and access control. If an end system does not pass all of the endpoint security checks and access is restricted, the user may be presented with a limited portal.

Some advanced products also have the capability to allow users to control the layout and customization of their own portals. This includes creating bookmarks, adding icons, and saving passwords.

3.3.4 Authentication

SSL VPNs support the authentication security service either directly through an integrated authentication method, or indirectly via an external authentication server, or both. Traditional SSL Web page authentication relies on server-side authentication, so that users trust the server with which they are communicating. SSL VPN authentication takes this a step further by requiring both server-side and client-side authentication. SSL VPNs support flexible client authentication methods, such as username and password, smart cards, two-factor authentication, and X.509 digital certificates. For the use of methods involving tokens, the SSL VPN must be able to handle the various messages, such as PIN change requests, that are involved in token solutions.

When digital certificates are used for client authentication, each endpoint has its own digital certificate that contains a public key. An endpoint uses the corresponding private key to digitally sign data before sending it to the other endpoint, which verifies the signature using the peer's public key. The digital signature algorithm choices are RSA and the Digital Signature Standard (DSS). In addition to authentication with certificates, the SSL VPN should also support certificate revocation list (CRL) checking. The SSL VPN should be able to generate certificate-signing requests for its own digital certificates. Note that most SSL VPNs that allow digital certificates for client authentication do so using proprietary mechanisms; this is because client digital certificate authentication often does not work well in typical Web browsers, which provide a difficult user interface for users who have many client certificates issued for different purposes.

In addition to the authentication methods already mentioned, SSL VPNs also support integration with external authentication servers such as RADIUS, Active Directory, and Lightweight Directory Access Protocol (LDAP), allowing the VPNs to leverage existing authentication databases. SSL VPNs need access to group information on the authentication servers since security and access control are often expressed in terms of groups. Some SSL VPN products also use the information contained in authentication servers to make additional access control decisions, such as restricting the number of bad password attempts. Windows Active Directory (AD) is a common type of authentication server that can be accessed directly or by using LDAP. Some SSL VPN products do not support direct AD authentication. To access AD via LDAP, the administrator must have strong knowledge of the underlying structure of the directory. In this case, it is easier and less time consuming to use an SSL VPN with the capability to communicate directly with AD.

SSL VPN authentication methods may be applied on an individual or group basis. One class of users may use a specific form of authentication and another class may use a different form of authentication. For example, employees may authenticate via username and password, and business partners may authenticate via digital certificates. Some SSL VPN products have the capability to combine various forms of authentication methods, such as using a digital certificate in addition to a username and password. Because integration with authentication servers is an area where SSL VPN products vary greatly, potential products should be evaluated with an organization's authentication servers to verify interoperability.

3.3.5 Encryption and Integrity Protection

SSL VPNs use the underlying SSL protocol to protect the confidentiality of data using encryption and to provide data integrity (ensuring that the data has not been modified). SSL VPN's encryption and data integrity come from SSL itself, not from any feature added by the SSL VPN product. SSL ensures the encryption and data integrity between the user's computer and the VPN gateway. Many SSL VPNs also support using SSL between the gateway and Web hosts on the protected network for applications that require encryption and integrity protection even within the protected network.

3.3.6 Access Control

SSL VPN products vary greatly in their access control features. Some products have an *allow* policy for the entire system by default, which allows authenticated users complete unrestricted access to the protected network. This may be adequate for a wide open network, but in most SSL VPN implementations, the organization will be providing different services to different types of users and will want controlled access. Granular access control supports one of the fundamental goals of SSL VPNs: to provide access to a variety of groups and users such as mobile employees, branch offices, business partners, and customers. Some SSL VPN products allow highly granular access control, which can include the particular application or file being accessed, day and time, type of browser, authentication method used, computer type and location, user identification, and other characteristics. The SSL VPN uses an access control policy to provide different services based on these characteristics.

Table 3-1 provides examples of typical access control policies. Access privileges may be granted to individuals, groups, or resources. For ease of configuration, access control is typically configured based on groups. Each user is assigned to one or more groups, each group having certain security parameters. Group information may be accessed from the authentication database, such as the LDAP directory. Access control may also be defined for a set of resources instead of an individual resource. This makes adding and removing resources to and from a group transparent to the users and reduces policy complexity. In some specific instances, user-level parameters are also set.

Table 3-1. Access Control Examples

Method	Example
Per-user	The CEO may access all intranet servers, email, and the executive folder of the administrative server.
Per-group	Sales staff may access email, the organization's intranet, and the sales server.
Per-resource	All users and groups may access the Community Relations server.

Access control can also be integrated with endpoint security controls. SSL VPNs can use host integrity checking to check the status of the SSL VPN client before access is granted. Some SSL VPNs have the capability to perform this checking either before or after authentication to determine the appropriate access controls. Access control in this sense may be as simple as allowing or denying access completely, or more elaborate such as providing restricted access to selected information based on host integrity checks. Access controls may also be configured per-user, per-group, and per-resource in terms of host integrity checking. It is beneficial to have the ability to bypass the endpoint security restrictions for certain circumstances such as disaster response. Bypassing endpoint security for special circumstances may be accomplished through a special access control policy setting or whitelist.

Table 3-2 shows some examples of access control policies in conjunction with endpoint security controls. These examples are an extension of the examples in Table 3-1. The first user is the CEO, who is accessing the SSL VPN from home via an organization-issued laptop. The firewall and antivirus software pass the security checks since they are enabled and up-to-date. Based on user and group access policies, and the passing of the endpoint security checks, the CEO may access the intranet servers, email, the executive folder of the administrative server, and the Community Relations server. The next user is John Smith, who is a traveling member of the sales team. He is attempting to access the SSL VPN from a public computer in an Internet café. The firewall passes the security checks, but the antivirus software is not up-to-date on its signatures. Based on user and group access policies and the fact that only some of the security checks passed, John is granted access to email and the ability to download (but not upload) files from the sales server (he would have been given more privileges if he had passed all the security checks). He may also access the Community Relations server. The last user is Sally Jones, who is an employee at a business partner, XYZ Corp. She is attempting to access the SSL VPN from a trusted partner network. Based on user and group access policies, and the passing of the endpoint security checks, Sally is granted access to the extranet partner server and the Community Relations server.

Table 3-2. Access Control Examples with Endpoint Security Controls

User	Group	Location	Security Checks	Access
CEO	• Executive • Employees	Home	Firewall: passed Antivirus: passed	The CEO may access all intranet servers, email, and the executive folder of the administrative server. He may also access the Community Relations server.
John Smith	• Sales • Employees	Internet café	Firewall: passed Antivirus: *failed*	John Smith may only access email and perform downloads from the sales server. He may also access the Community Relations server.
Sally Jones	• XYZ Corp. (Business Partner)	Partner network	Firewall: passed Antivirus: passed	Sally Jones may access the extranet partner server and the Community Relations server.

Knowing the needs and requirements for the SSL VPN solution, such as the types of users and the reasons they will use the SSL VPN, will help organizations choose a product with the appropriate level of access control capability. These needs and requirements will also help organizations determine the level of granularity needed for access controls.

3.3.7 Endpoint Security Controls

Some SSL VPNs provide endpoint security controls that include host integrity checking and security protection mechanisms. Host integrity checks help ensure that the client system is in compliance with an organization's security policy. These checks are performed before a session is begun and may be periodically rechecked during the session.

Endpoint security controls are sometimes tightly integrated with access control to analyze the client system and apply access controls based on the results. For example, an up-to-date company-issued laptop that is connecting from a remote site might be allowed full access. Another example is a personal laptop that complies with the standard firewall and antivirus checks but is attempting access from an untrusted wireless hotspot, and thus is granted only limited access. Endpoint security controls also include security protection mechanisms, such as Web browser cache cleaners that remove temporary files, cookies, and other session information from the Web browser used for SSL VPN access. This supports the use of the SSL VPN from public locations.

Endpoint security controls can be implemented in a variety of ways, and this often differentiates products. Endpoint security starts with a policy definition. The policy definition includes what the host integrity checker should look for and the actions to take depending on what it finds. If host integrity checkers are used, they should be configured to execute before the logon process to look for malware such as keystroke loggers. Typical host integrity checks may look for operating system type and version, antivirus and personal firewall status and configurations, or a specific file, registry key, or running process. Depending on the product, checking for running processes may be as simple as looking for the process name or as elaborate as verifying the actual validity of the process.

Some SSL VPN products include their own integrated endpoint security software. This software may be part of the SSL VPN product or an add-on for an additional cost. Other SSL VPN products rely on third-party software for endpoint security. This allows organizations to leverage their existing products, such as cache cleaning tools, malware scanners, and compliance checking software, with their SSL VPNs. Some of these SSL VPNs can only integrate with a single specific third-party product, while others can integrate with a variety of third-party products.

Some SSL VPN products provide endpoint security controls for systems that are connecting into the network via the network extension function. Such systems are generally of higher concern than those that are just accessing Web sites, since these systems are usually granted much broader access to resources.

Endpoint security controls should be used with care. Due to the nature of remote access, the client systems are more likely to be originating from uncontrolled environments. It is imperative that remote systems are evaluated before allowing access to internal resources and cleaned after access is granted. There is no industry-wide standard for endpoint security controls; many leading network and security companies are working to create vendor-driven standards.

3.3.8 Intrusion Prevention

Some SSL VPN products provide an integrated intrusion prevention security service. They inspect the contents of the data after it has been decrypted by the SSL VPN for potential attacks and various forms of malware, including viruses and worms. The SSL VPN may include its own anti-malware and intrusion detection software, or it may integrate with third-party software. Performing content inspection adds processing time and latency to the throughput of packets. For high-volume networks, this latency in addition to the latency of the encryption and decryption process may exceed tolerable limits. In those cases, it is best to offload the intrusion prevention capabilities to a specialized intrusion prevention system (IPS) device on the inside of the trusted network (that is, after the SSL VPN has decrypted the data).

3.4 SSL Protocol Basics

The security of the data sent over an SSL VPN relies on the security of the SSL protocol. The SSL protocol allows a client (such as a Web browser) and a server (such as an SSL VPN) to negotiate the type of security to be used during an SSL session. Thus, it is critical to make sure that the security agreed to by the remote user and the SSL gateway meets the security requirements of the organization using the SSL VPN.

There are three types of security that the client and server can negotiate: the version of SSL, the type of cryptography, and the authentication method. All three are important to the security of the communications channel that is established and are thus important to SSL VPN systems. These are discussed in more detail in Sections 3.4.1 through 3.4.3.

NIST Special Publication (SP) 800-52, *Guidelines for the Selection and Use of Transport Layer Security (TLS) Implementations*[6], describes the technology used in SSL and TLS in detail. Readers of this document who want to know more about these technologies are encouraged to read that publication.

3.4.1 Versions of SSL and TLS

In this document, the terms *SSL* and *TLS* are often used together to describe the same protocol. In fact, SSL refers to all versions of the SSL protocol as defined by the IETF, while TLS refers only to versions 3.1 and later of the SSL protocol. Two versions of TLS have been standardized: TLS 1.0 and TLS 1.1. TLS 1.0 is the same as SSL 3.1; there are no versions of SSL after 3.1. As of the writing of this guide, work is being done on TLS version 1.2. TLS is approved for use in the protection of Federal information; SSL versions other than 3.1 are not.

Different SSL VPNs and different Web browsers use different versions of the SSL and TLS protocols. For example, some browsers support SSL 3.0 but not TLS 1.0 or 1.1; other browsers support TLS 1.0 but

---

[6] For more information see NIST SP 800-52, *Guidelines for the Selection and Use of Transport Layer Security (TLS)*, at http://csrc.nist.gov/publications/nistpubs/.

not SSL 3.0. Because each version of SSL or TLS is incompatible with other versions, both the browser and the SSL VPN have to have at least one version of SSL in common. Further, they both have to have a version in common that meets the security policy of the organization running the SSL VPN; otherwise, the browser and the SSL VPN gateway will not be able to communicate.

3.4.2 Cryptography Used in SSL Sessions

There are many types of cryptographic functions that are used in security protocols. The most widely known cryptographic features are *confidentiality* (secrecy of data), *integrity* (the ability to detect even minute changes in the data), and *signature* (the ability to trace the origin of the data). The combination of these features is an important aspect of the overall security of a communications stream. SSL uses four significant types of features: confidentiality, integrity, signature, and *key establishment* (the way that a key is agreed to by the two parties).

SSL uses *cipher suites* to define the set of cryptographic functions that a client and server use when communicating. This is unlike protocols such as IPsec and S/MIME where the two parties agree to individual cryptographic functions. That is, SSL exchanges say in effect, "Here is a set of functions to be used together, and here is another set I am willing to use." IPsec and S/MIME (and many other protocols) instead say, "Here are the confidentiality functions I am willing to use, here are the integrity functions I am willing to use, and here are the signature algorithms I am willing to use", and the other side creates a set from those choices.

Just as the SSL client and server need to be able to use the same version of SSL, they also need to be able to use the same cipher suite; otherwise, the two sides cannot communicate. The organization running the SSL VPN chooses which cipher suites meet its security goals and configures the SSL VPN gateway to use only those cipher suites.

3.4.3 Authentication Used for Identifying SSL Servers

When a Web browser connects to an SSL server such as an SSL VPN gateway, the browser user needs some way to know that the browser is talking to a server the user trusts. SSL uses certificates that are signed by trusted entities to authenticate the server to the Web user. (SSL can also use certificates to authenticate users to servers, but this is rarely done.)

The server authentication occurs very early in the SSL process, immediately after the user sends its first message to the SSL server. In that first message, the Web browser specifies which type of certificate algorithms it can handle; the two common choices are RSA and DSS. In the second message, the SSL server responds with a certificate of one of the types that the browser said it understands. After receiving the certificate, the Web browser verifies that the identity in the certificate (that is, the domain name listed in the certificate) matches the domain name to which the Web browser attempted to connect.

Some SSL VPNs use certificates issued by the vendor of the SSL VPN, and those certificates do not link through a chain of trust to a root certificate that is normally trusted by most users. If that is the case, the user should add the SSL VPN's own certificate to the user's list of directly-trusted certificates. It is important to note that users should not add the root certificate of the SSL VPN's manufacturer to the list of certification authorities that the user trusts, since the manufacturer's security policies and controls may differ from those of the organization. Other SSL VPNs produce self-signed certificates that do not chain to any trusted root certificate; as before, the user should add the SSL VPN's own certificate to the user's list of directly-trusted certificates.

Certificates are signed with keys of a specified length. The security of the authentication is linked to the length of the key that is protecting the identity in the certificate. If an SSL server uses a key of insufficient length to protect its identity, the Web client might not want to trust the identity at all. In most Web browsers, there are mechanisms to check the length of the key that was used by the SSL server after the browser has successfully made an SSL connection.

3.5 SSL VPN Challenges

SSL VPNs are rapidly maturing technologies. Nevertheless, they still face several challenges:

- **Application and client interoperability**. This is the biggest challenge for SSL VPNs. SSL VPNs must be able to export a large variety of applications to remote connections of various types. There are many factors that can affect interoperability, including operating system type and version, browser type and version, device type (e.g., laptop, PDA, smart phone), location (e.g., home or public kiosk), and the specifics of the applications and protocols to be accessed. For example, some SSL VPN products offer support for PDAs, but most offer limited (if any) support for smart phones. Some SSL VPN devices support phones via a browser, for web-based access, but few support them from an agent perspective, allowing access to client/server applications.

- **Client/server application support**. SSL VPNs are also still struggling with client/server applications. Some VPNs use application translation and network extension, along with special clients, to establish the appropriate access. Each SSL VPN product that uses network extension tends to have a unique solution to client/server applications. In addition, not all SSL VPN products support the same applications; some support more than others and each has niche areas.

- **Network extension**. Although the network extension function is a core part of SSL tunnel VPNs, it still presents several challenges. Network extension requires a client to be installed on the end user's system. Installing this client on a public kiosk or on a PC that has policies against downloading programs and plug-ins may not be possible due to insufficient privileges. Because network extension gives a remote user complete access to internal systems, specific per-application access controls may be difficult to enforce.

- **Endpoint security**. Endpoint security for unmanaged PCs and public computers also remains a challenge. Two issues are trusting the endpoint responses to the host integrity checks and performing proper sanitization of sensitive information from the client system when the session is terminated. Unmanaged public client systems are less likely to have antivirus and firewall software enabled and up-to-date. A compromised public computer could trick the host integrity checks by circumventing them or by simulating firewalls, antivirus software, and other required security controls. The systems are also more likely to be infected with malware, such as Trojan horses and keystroke loggers, that could gain access to passwords and other sensitive information. In addition, proper sanitization of these systems after the session terminates often requires elevated privileges.

- **Clientless operation**. SSL VPNs are often described as being clientless, which is used as a selling point over traditional IPsec VPNs. For Web-enabled applications, the Web browser is the only client piece needed to connect to them via an SSL portal VPN. In other cases, dynamically downloaded agents, which may require software installation, are needed to provide access to legacy and client/server applications and network layer connections to non-Web enabled applications; these are the hallmarks of SSL tunnel VPNs. Proper privileges are needed to install the software and make appropriate system configurations. This has caused much debate in the security community over the marketing of SSL tunnel VPNs as clientless. In the cases where dynamic agents are necessary, some systems and locations, such as public kiosks, may be unable to install the appropriate software or use the SSL VPN.

3.6 Summary

SSL VPNs can support a range of users, on a variety of computers, accessing resources from many locations. They can provide secure remote access to internal services such as email, file servers, and other applications in a Web-based format. SSL VPNs use the SSL protocol, which is included in all standard Web browsers, to secure the transmission of data between the user and the organization as it traverses public networks.

SSL VPNs consist of three core functions to enable secure access to internal resources. These functions—proxying, application translation, and network extension—provide multiple methods to enable remote access to a variety of applications. This allows SSL VPNs to support Web-based, client/server, and legacy applications. Proxying provides the simplest form of an SSL VPN by enabling encryption and authentication for internal Web sites. Application translation is often used to access non-Web-enabled applications by converting a legacy or proprietary protocol into a more widely used or standard protocol. Network extension provides complete network access to remote users as if they were physically located on the internal local area network. Users with network extension can access all network resources, not just Web servers; this is particularly useful in organizations with custom applications that cannot be translated to the Web easily.

SSL VPNs vary in breadth, depth, and completeness of features and security services. This makes it important to identify and define requirements, and evaluate several products to determine their fit into the organization. Recommendations and considerations include the following:

- Because some SSL VPN products cannot cover all remote access needs, for selecting the best product it is recommended to identify the remote access needs and the applications that require remote access.

- Each SSL VPN supports different protocols via proxy and application translation. In addition, some SSL VPN products have concentrated their efforts and expertise in supporting certain protocols and applications. It is crucial to make sure that the SSL VPN provides the necessary proxies and application translators for the applications that require remote access.

- SSL VPN manageability features such as status reporting, logging, and auditing should provide adequate capabilities for the organization to effectively operate and manage the SSL VPN and to extract detailed usage information.

- The SSL VPN high availability and scalability features should support the organization's requirements for failover, load balancing, and throughput. State and information sharing is recommended to keep the failover process transparent to the user.

- SSL VPN portal customization should allow the organization to control the look and feel of the portal and to customize the portal to support various devices such as PDAs and smart phones.

- SSL VPN authentication should provide the necessary support for the organization's current and future authentication methods and to leverage existing authentication databases. SSL VPN authentication should also be tested to ensure interoperability with existing authentication methods.

- Some organizations, such as Federal agencies, have strict requirements for encryption and integrity protection. SSL VPNs should support the required algorithms for symmetric encryption, key exchange, and hash functions. All cryptographic algorithms and modules must be FIPS-approved.

- SSL VPNs should be evaluated to ensure they provide the level of granularity needed for access controls. Access controls should be capable of applying permissions to users, groups, and resources, as well as integrating with endpoint security controls.

- Implementation of endpoint security controls varies greatly from one SSL VPN product to another. Endpoint security should be evaluated to ensure it provides the necessary host integrity checking and security protection mechanisms for the organization.

- Not all SSL VPNs have integrated intrusion prevention capabilities. Those that do should be evaluated to ensure they do not introduce an unacceptable amount of latency into the network traffic.

Several of the security services provided by SSL VPNs rely on the underlying SSL protocol. SSL VPNs may use versions of either SSL or TLS protocols. The choice of which protocol to implement depends on the data being secured. For example, TLS is approved for use in the protection of Federal information; SSL versions other than 3.1 are not. The SSL VPN must be configured to ensure that the appropriate protocol is used. This also applies to the security mechanisms that SSL and TLS use to secure communications.

Not all SSL VPN products include all of these services, and there are differences in the level of sophistication of the services that are supported. The main differentiators for SSL VPN products are how they implement security policies and handle remote clients, and how transparent their usage is to the end user. The strengths of an SSL VPN include support for a variety of systems and locations, granular access control, Web browser client access, and ease of use.

SSL VPNs, although a maturing technology, continue to face several challenges. These include limitations on their ability to support a large number of applications and clients, the methods of implementing network extension and endpoint security, the ability to provide clientless access, the use of the SSL VPN from public locations, and product and technology education.

4. SSL VPN Planning and Implementation

This section focuses on the planning and implementation of SSL VPNs in the enterprise. As with any new technology deployment, SSL VPN planning and implementation should be addressed in a phased approach. A successful SSL VPN deployment can be achieved by following a clear, step-by-step planning and implementation process. The use of a phased approach can minimize unforeseen issues and identify potential pitfalls early in the process. This section explores in depth each of the recommended SSL VPN planning and implementation phases, as follows:

1. **Identify Requirements.** The first phase of the process involves identifying the current and future requirements for remote access and determining how they can best be met by an SSL VPN implementation. Determining requirements for U.S. federal agencies also means assessing how to comply with FIPS 140-2.

2. **Design the Solution.** The second phase involves all aspects of designing an SSL VPN solution. The design elements are grouped into five categories: access control, endpoint security, authentication methods, architecture, and cryptography policy.

3. **Implement and Test a Prototype.** The next phase involves implementing and testing a prototype in a laboratory or test environment. The primary goals are to evaluate all aspects of the solution including authentication, application compatibility, management, logging, performance, security of the implementation, design and layout of the VPN portal, and default settings.

4. **Deploy the Solution.** Once testing is completed and all issues are resolved, the next phase includes the deployment of the SSL VPN throughout the enterprise. This phase addresses issues specific to SSL VPNs that may occur during deployment. Support must be addressed, and this includes the process of working with a help desk to provide assistance for end users.

5. **Manage the Solution.** After the SSL VPN solution has been deployed, it must be managed throughout its lifecycle. Management includes maintenance (e.g., patching, solution expansion, key management, policy changes), performance monitoring, and periodic testing/validation of the solution. The handling of operational issues must also be considered.

Organizations should also put into place other measures that support and complement SSL VPN implementations. These measures help to ensure that the SSL VPN solution is implemented in an environment with the technical, management, and operational controls necessary to provide sufficient security for the SSL VPN. Examples of supporting measures include:

- Establish and maintain control over all entry and exit points for the protected network to help ensure its integrity.

- Ensure that all SSL VPN endpoints are secured and maintained properly to reduce the risk of SSL VPN compromise or misuse.

4.1 Identify Requirements

The purpose of this phase is to identify which resources or services need to be available for remote access and who should be able to access them through the SSL VPN. It is also important to identify other general and application-specific requirements, such as performance, and to think about future requirements. For example, if it is likely that other resources will need to be accessible by remote users in a year, then those needs should also be considered.

One of the primary strengths of an SSL VPN architecture is its granularity of access control. An organization should leverage this feature by being specific in its identification of resources, the users who can access them, and other security requirements. It is helpful to begin this process by articulating a set of organizational requirements for remote access. These requirements are not strictly technical but are dictated by the needs of the organization. Here are a few examples of organizational requirements:

- All employees should be able to access the main corporate applications and a set of Web-based applications such as email that are all hosted on the intranet servers.

- A small group of executives should be able to access the executive file share on the administrative server.

- The sales team should have access to the sales database and the sales file share on the sales server.

- Business partners should be able to access the extranet partner server.

- Network administrators should have full access to routers, switches, and other network infrastructure (network management devices, etc.)

The next step is to determine other requirements such as anticipated performance requirements (normal and peak loads), service level agreement (SLA) guarantees, and the use of multiple languages.

The organization should consider the best possible technical solution once its requirements are identified. It is possible that other protocols such as SSH or IPsec provide a better technical solution than SSL. This is especially pertinent if a VPN solution already exists, because it could potentially be leveraged to meet the identified requirements. See Section 6 for descriptions of such protocols and guidance on when a particular protocol may be a viable alternative to SSL. SSL may be the only option in some cases, such as when granularity on a per-application basis is required for remote access or if the VPN needs to be available to remote users without any software or hardware installation.

4.2 SSL VPNs and FIPS 140-2 Approval

Federal agencies are required to use cryptographic algorithms that are NIST-approved and contained in FIPS-validated modules. The FIPS 140-2[7] specification defines how cryptographic modules will be validated. One requirement of FIPS 140 is that the module be capable of operating in a mode where all algorithms are NIST-approved. NIST-approved algorithms are specified in a FIPS (e.g., FIPS 180, *Secure Hash Standard*[8]) or in a NIST Recommendation (e.g., SP 800-56A, *Recommendation for Pair-Wise Key Establishment Schemes Using Discrete Logarithm Cryptography*[9]). Where there are no NIST-approved algorithms in a specific class, such as key transport, the Cryptographic Module Validation Program (CMVP) Implementation Guidance may specify additional constraints. Because SSL VPN technology employs a number of cryptographic algorithms, Federal agencies must be aware of whether their chosen SSL VPN technology is FIPS-compliant now and whether it is expected to be FIPS-compliant during the entire expected lifetime of the system.

Many of the cryptographic algorithms used in some SSL cipher suites are not FIPS-approved, and therefore are not allowed for use in SSL VPNs that are to be used in applications that must conform to

---

[7] For more information on FIPS PUB 140-2, *Security Requirements for Cryptographic Modules,* please refer to http://csrc.nist.gov/publications/PubsFIPS.html. Information on the Cryptographic Module Validation program can be found at http://csrc.nist.gov/groups/STM/cmvp/index.html.
[8] The latest version of FIPS 180, FIPS 180-3, can be found at http://csrc.nist.gov/publications/PubsFIPS.html.
[9] SP 800-56A can be found at http://csrc.nist.gov/publications/PubsSPs.html.

FIPS 140-2. This means that to be run in FIPS-compliant mode, an SSL VPN gateway must only allow cipher suites that are allowed by FIPS 140-2.

NIST SP 800-52[10] lists the TLS cipher suites that satisfied FIPS requirements as of its publication date (June 2005); additional cipher suites meeting FIPS requirements may become available in the future. All of the cipher suites listed in SP 800-52 will become disallowed after the end of 2010. Therefore, Federal agencies who want to provide SSL VPN services after 2010 must ensure that their systems are upgradeable to the new FIPS-compliant cipher suites before the end of 2010, and that their SSL VPN vendors guarantee that such upgrades will be available early enough for testing and deployment in the field. Further, those systems must be able to be configured to *only* use cipher suites with FIPS-compliant hash functions. Otherwise, a client that is offering a cipher suite with non-compliant cryptographic functions might negotiate an SSL session that does not rely on FIPS-compliant technologies.

4.2.1 Versions of SSL

Because of the way that SSL was designed, SSL versions 3.0 and earlier do not conform to the requirements of FIPS 140-2. Therefore, SSL VPNs that are to be used in applications that must be FIPS-compliant must use TLS 1.0 (SSL 3.1) or later for their SSL VPN systems. Further, those systems must be able to be configured to *only* use TLS 1.0 or later; otherwise, a client that is using SSL 3.0 or earlier might use the SSL negotiation to cause the SSL VPN gateway to create an SSL session that is inappropriate for the security level of the organization. A client that only uses SSL 3.0 or earlier should not be permitted to establish an SSL VPN connection; nevertheless, few SSL VPNs have the capability to enforce this restriction.

4.2.2 Key Establishment Used by SSL

NIST SP 800-56A[11], *Recommendation for Pair-Wise Key Establishment Schemes Using Discrete Logarithm Cryptography*, defines the types of key establishment algorithms that can be used in FIPS-compliant systems that use cryptography such as Diffie-Hellman key exchange. As described in NIST SP 800-52, the method for key establishment in SSL version 3.1 and later that is preferred by NIST is *ephemeral Diffie-Hellman*.

The ephemeral Diffie-Hellman key establishment used by TLS version 1.0 and later does not meet the requirements of NIST SP 800-56A. NIST has granted a special exception from this requirement for systems using SSL until the end of 2010; see *Implementation Guidance for FIPS PUB 140-2 and the Cryptographic Module Validation Program*[12]. Subject to the results of further analysis, the date may be extended. SSL's RSA key establishment method, which is not covered by the restrictions in NIST SP 800-56A, is acceptable now and beyond 2010.

Therefore, purchasers of SSL VPNs who need to be FIPS-compliant after the end of 2010 must ensure that their SSL VPN systems can be configured to require RSA key establishment at that time. Until that time, SSL VPN systems can also use the NIST-preferred method of ephemeral Diffie-Hellman.

---

[10] For more information see NIST SP 800-52, *Guidelines for the Selection and Use of Transport Layer Security (TLS)*, at http://csrc.nist.gov/publications/nistpubs.
[11] For more information on NIST SP 800-56A, *Recommendation for Pair-Wise Key Establishment Schemes Using Discrete Logarithm Cryptography*, refer to http://csrc.nist.gov/publications/nistpubs.
[12] For more information, refer to http://csrc.nist.gov/groups/STM/cmvp/documents/fips140-2/FIPS1402IG.pdf.

4.2.3 Hash Functions Used by SSL

SSL VPN devices that are to be used in FIPS-compliant applications must also use FIPS-compliant hash functions. Plain SHA-1 can only be used until the end of 2010 in FIPS-compliant systems[13]. The keyed-hash message authentication code (HMAC) form of SHA-1 is still considered secure, and can be used after 2010. Since SSL VPN devices use HMAC-SHA-1, those suites that employ this hash function will remain acceptable beyond 2010.

4.2.4 SSL Encryption

SSL VPN devices that are to be used in FIPS-compliant applications must use FIPS-compliant encryption. Fortunately, virtually all SSL VPN devices can do this. Further, those systems must be able to be configured to *only* use cipher suites with FIPS-compliant encryption; otherwise, a client that is offering a cipher suite with non-compliant encryption might use the SSL negotiation to cause the SSL VPN gateway to create an SSL session that is inappropriate for the security level of the organization.

Some SSL VPN devices can be configured to only allow certain cipher suites, or at least to only allow cipher suites with certain types of encryption. Other SSL VPN devices do not allow such configuration. NIST SP 800-52 lists the types of encryption that satisfied FIPS requirements when it was published (June 2005); additional encryption algorithms meeting FIPS requirements may become available in the future.

4.2.5 Certificates Used During SSL Negotiations

Finally, FIPS compliance for SSL VPNs requires the use of FIPS-compliant key sizes and hash functions for signatures in the certificates used for authentication. Fortunately, virtually all SSL VPN devices are able to do this today. Further, those systems must be able to be configured to *only* use FIPS-compliant key sizes and hash functions in these certificates; otherwise, a client or server whose certificate uses a non-compliant key size or hash function might use the SSL negotiation to cause the SSL VPN gateway to create an SSL session that is inappropriate for the security level of the organization.

Note that the list of allowed hash functions will change at the end of 2010. After that time, server certificates that use the SHA-1 hash function will no longer be allowed, and all FIPS-compliant SSL VPN devices will need to use certificates that use the SHA-256 hash function. Some SSL VPN devices today cannot use such certificates as the server authenticating certificate. Further, not all Web browsers today support certificates that use the SHA-256 hash function for authentication.

SSL server authentication certificates can use either the RSA or DSS signature schemes, although many SSL VPN systems and most Web browsers only support RSA. Note that if a server authenticates itself with a Digital Signature Algorithm (DSA) certificate, the key negotiation must use the ephemeral Diffie-Hellman method. That method is not allowed to be used after the end of 2010, and therefore SSL VPN systems that use DSA certificates cannot be used after the end of 2010 unless the special exception allowing the use of ephemeral Diffie-Hellman for SSL key establishment is extended. For DSA, a FIPS 186-3[14] compliant digital signature is required for the larger key sizes.

At the current time, few (if any) SSL VPN gateways can be configured to reject certificates based on the size of the key used and therefore most can be used in FIPS-noncompliant modes without any way to prevent such use. Worse, few (if any) SSL VPN gateways even log the size of the key used in certificate

---

[13] For more information, see http://csrc.nist.gov/groups/ST/hash/policy.html and http://csrc.nist.gov/groups/ST/hash/statement.html.
[14] FIPS 186-3, *Digital Signature Standard (DSS)*, can be found at http://csrc.nist.gov/publications/PubsFIPS.html.

authentication, so it is not possible to audit which sessions are FIPS-compliant. Worse yet, few (if any) SSL VPN browsers can be configured to reject server certificates based on the size of the key used and therefore most can be used in FIPS-noncompliant modes without any way to prevent such use.

To guarantee FIPS compliance, SSL VPNs that cannot enforce requiring particular key sizes need to be configured with both of the following settings:

- The server certificate used for authenticating the SSL VPN device to clients must have an appropriate-length key.

- One of the following steps must be performed:

  - The SSL VPN gateway must be configured to only validate client certificates that have a certificate policy that enforces the key size requirement.

  - The SSL VPN gateway must be configured to only validate client certificates from a pre-approved list. (In this way, key size validation can be handled at the time the client certificate is registered.)

  - The use of client certificates for authentication to the SSL VPN gateway must be disabled. In place of client certificates, a smartcard or token should be used. If that is not possible, a username and password may be used, but this solution is a last resort and its use is discouraged.

It is important to note that the minimum FIPS-compliant key length for DSA and RSA certificates will change at the end of 2010 from 1024 bits to 2048 bits; see *Implementation Guidance for FIPS PUB 140-2 and the Cryptographic Module Validation Program* for more information.

4.3 Design the Solution

Once the requirements have been identified, and it has been determined that an SSL VPN is the best solution, the next phase is to design a solution that meets the specified requirements. This phase is broken into five major components that are described in more detail in the following subsections.

- **Access Control.** Design the access control policy. SSL VPN users may gain access to particular resources based on characteristics such as user identification, computer type and location, and the method of authentication.

- **Endpoint Security.** Design the endpoint security controls. SSL VPNs provide endpoint security controls that include host integrity checking and security protection mechanisms. Host integrity checks ensure that the client system is in compliance with an organization's minimum security policy. Typical host integrity checks may look for operating system type and version, antivirus and personal firewall status and configurations, or a specific file, registry key, or process that is running.

- **Authentication.** Select the authentication methods. There are many ways to authenticate SSL VPN users, including LDAP, RADIUS, Active Directory, and digital certificates.

- **Architecture.** Designing the architecture of the SSL VPN implementation includes hardware selection, device placement, firewall and routing considerations, client software selection, high availability configuration, and portal design.

- **Cryptography Policy and FIPS Compliance.** The organization must choose a cryptography policy that fits its needs and is compliant with its requirements. In addition, Federal agencies must use only cryptographic modules that have algorithms and methods that are compliant with the FIPS 140-2 specification.

4.3.1 Design the Access Control Policy

After the organization determines what resources will be accessible and by whom, the next step is to design the access control policy. The organization should base this policy on the organizational requirements that were identified in the Identify Requirements phase. These requirements stipulate which resources should be accessed by which groups or individuals. The access control policy could provide additional requirements and make access to resources dependent on other characteristics such as the authentication method used, computer type and location, and user identification.

The four major steps in designing an access control policy are as follows:

1. **List the resources that will be accessed through the SSL VPN.** A resource is as specific as a single application on one server or as general as an enterprise-wide service such as email or all internal Web sites. Resources can be treated separately or grouped together. For example, one specific human resources application can be listed by itself or grouped with a collection of other human resources applications. A resource can be a member of more than one group, but grouping in this way should not be used extensively because security holes or other problems can be created. For example, if Application X is a member of Groups A and B, a user that is granted access to Group A but denied access to Group B may still have access to Application X.

2. **List the groups or users.** An access control policy is much more manageable if users are assigned primarily to groups. A user can be a member of more than one group. For example, an executive is a member of the Executive and Employee groups, and a salesperson is a member of the Sales and Employee groups.

3. **List the conditions under which the resources should be accessible by the groups.** Conditions are based on the ability of endpoint security controls to perform host integrity checking on the client hosts. Host integrity checking, which is discussed in more detail in Section 4.3.2, involves performing checks on conditions, including the type of operating system on the client machine, the presence of a firewall or antivirus scanner, registry settings, authentication method used, and time of day. These conditions will help determine what resources are accessible by the user. For example, users logging in from an organization-managed host would have access to more resources than if they were to log in from a public system at an Internet café.

4. **List how the VPN should be used to access the resources.** As mentioned in Section 3.2, there are three main components to SSL VPNs: proxying, application translation, and network extension. Proxying is most often used to provide secure access to Web sites. Application translation uses proxying to translate an application into a format that is Web-enabled and accessible through a browser. Finally, network extension provides broad access to the internal network. The organization should decide how each resource should be accessed through the VPN. Proxying and application translation offer the most restrictive access because all communication takes place through the browser interface. Network extension is the easiest to use because users have full network access, but it should be used with discretion for this reason.

A limited type of network extension, *port forwarding*, is sometimes used instead of full network extension. Port forwarding only creates tunnels for certain TCP or UDP ports instead of for all ports at one time. For example, a port forwarding system might tunnel HTTP traffic but not DNS traffic, leaving the DNS traffic outside of the VPN. Because port forwarding technology is a subset of network extension, this document discusses only network extension.

Most SSL VPN devices offer packet filtering for users that access resources via network extension. Because network extension provides broad access to users, the most effective way to protect certain subnets may be to configure packet filters that prevent access to them. SSL VPN devices may also support multiple routing tables for users. One routing table can be used to provide access to all internal subnets, while another routing table enables connectivity to subnets that only specific groups should access.

The following is an example of an organization's access control requirements. The organizational requirements listed in the Identify Requirements phase are repeated here as a reminder:

- All employees should be able to access the main corporate applications and a set of Web-based applications such as email that are all hosted on the intranet servers.
- A small group of executives should be able to access the executive file share on the administrative server.
- The sales team should have access to the sales database and the sales file share on the sales server.
- Business partners should be able to access the extranet partner server.
- Network administrators should have full access to routers, switches, and other network infrastructure.

The resources that should be made accessible by the SSL VPN are then specified:

- Corporate applications on intranet servers (grouped together)
- Web applications—email and calendaring (grouped together)
- Executive file share on administrative server
- Sales database
- Sales file share on sales server
- Extranet partner server
- Network infrastructure devices (grouped together).

The groups that should be able to access resources are as follows:

- Employees
- Executives
- Sales
- Business partners
- Administrators.

These are the conditions by which resources can be accessed by groups:

- All employees should be able to access the main enterprise applications on the intranet servers from organization-managed hosts. An organization-managed host has a firewall, antivirus software, and a registry key indicating that it is managed by the organization.

- When these same users log in from any other host such as a PC at a kiosk or in an Internet café, they should be able to access only a limited set of Web-based applications such as email and calendaring. The only condition for *any host* is that, if it is running a Windows operating system, it must be using one or more specific versions of Windows, with each specific version using the most current set of updates.

- Executives have the same access rights as other employees, as well as access to the executive file share on the administrative server. The executives are only given this access from organization-managed hosts.

- Members of the sales group have the same access rights as other employees. In addition, they should have full access to the sales database and the sales file share on the sales server when they are using their own organization-managed hosts; from other hosts, they can only access the sales file share on the sales folder.

- Business partners should be able to access the extranet partner server from specified IP addresses only Monday to Friday between 9 a.m. and 5 p.m. Eastern time.

- In addition to all other resources, network administrators should have access to a range of subnets that are assigned to network infrastructure devices. They only have this access if they are using their organization-managed hosts.

Note that these conditions are not mutually exclusive and can be fulfilled simultaneously. So a user who logs in from an organization-managed host also satisfies the *any host* condition.

The organization has decided to use the following access types for the various resources:

- The corporate applications are accessible by network extension because there are a broad number of them on multiple servers. Access to routers, switches, and other network infrastructure are also accessible through network extension. Packet filtering is used to limit access to the specific application servers.

- The Web applications are accessible by proxy because they are already available by Web browser.

- The executive file share is accessible by proxying so that executives can use the file share in the same fashion whether connecting remotely or internally.

- The sales database is accessible by proxying because database administrators require direct access to the database server. The application is therefore not able to be translated.

- Both the sales file share and file shares on the extranet partner server are made accessible by translation, where all file sharing takes place in a Web browser.

Table 4-1 shows the resources and groups listed with conditions for access.

Table 4-1. Sample Access Control Policy

Resource	Group	Condition	Access Type
Corporate applications	Employees	Organization-managed host	Network extension
Web applications	Employees	Any host	Proxy
Executive file share	Executives	Organization-managed host	Proxy
Sales database	Sales	Organization-managed host	Proxy
Sales file share	Sales	Any host	Translation
Extranet partner server	Business Partners	Correct IP address and time	Translation
Network infrastructure	Administrators	Organization-managed host	Network extension

Users are added to the various groups to grant them access to resources via the SSL VPN. For example, regular employees are added to the Employees group, while executives are added to both the Executives and Employees groups. A user in the Employees group who logs in from an organization-managed host is granted access to both the corporate applications and Web applications resources. This same user is restricted to only Web applications if the host cannot be verified as organization-managed.

Note that the access policy is configured to restrict access to the executive file share only to users who belong to the Executives group and are logging in from an organization-managed host. An executive is only given the access privileges of a regular employee if he or she logs in from any other host. If desired, users could also use a different authentication method to receive access to the executive file share.

This access control policy assumes that a user can satisfy multiple conditions simultaneously. For example, a user who logs in from an organization-managed host also satisfies the *any host* condition and is granted access to the corresponding resources. If the SSL VPN device cannot support this flexibility, then the organization would have to specify the resources for each condition.

4.3.2 Design the Endpoint Security Policy

Once the organization designs its access control policy, it should consider constructing a policy to enforce endpoint security. Such a policy could initially verify that a client host complies with an organization's security policy by requiring host integrity checks to be performed on the client host. It is recommended to run the checks before the login process to look for malware such as keystroke loggers or viruses.

The checks can prohibit login altogether if the client host does not comply with the organization's minimum security policy. For example, the organization's endpoint security policy may specify that desktop search tools that index the contents of a user's hard drive are prohibited during an SSL VPN session because these tools can cache data from the session. If this is the case, then the host integrity checking process may either turn off the search tools directly or prevent login until the tools are explicitly turned off by the user.

Some SSL VPN vendors perform the host integrity checks by having the client host dynamically download active content from the SSL VPN device and then execute the active content. In this case, the client operating system and browser need to be configured to permit these agents to be downloaded and executed; otherwise, the client could perceive the agents as malware and block them, preventing the SSL VPN from performing the host integrity checks. This shows a basic conundrum of using this type of integrity check: some organizations prohibit such active content to be run in browsers because it is difficult to distinguish it from malware.

An endpoint security policy should also specify how to enforce endpoint security on a client system after the user has logged out. Security protection mechanisms such as a cache cleaner can be activated during the logout process to remove data that was cached or saved during the SSL VPN session. For even higher security, some SSL VPN vendors offer the capability of putting the session into a virtual storage space. The SSL VPN device allocates temporary memory and hard drive space for it. On a Windows machine, the virtual storage space may consist of temporary My Documents and Desktop directories. The user is not able to save anything to a directory outside of the virtual storage space. After the user logs out, the entire virtual storage space and all data downloaded during the session is erased. This virtual space may also be encrypted for greater security. Not all applications may be compatible with the virtual storage space because some of the user's directories are temporarily replaced, and interoperability problems could result. Also, the organization will have to make a policy decision about when to put users into the virtual storage space. For example, it may make sense to allow users to access their entire hard drive and keep downloaded files or email attachments if they are logging into the SSL VPN from their own organization-managed hosts.

If a user forgets to log out, the SSL VPN device should be able to perform an automatic logout after a specific period of inactivity. Ideally the device could detect and ignore activity that is automatic, such as an email client that periodically connects to the mail server or automatic refresh requests by a Web browser. The device may also have a separate timeout threshold to require re-authentication regardless of inactivity. This timeout limits the damage that is done if a malicious user somehow gets control of the VPN session. Some SSL VPN devices may have different timeout thresholds for different types of users. For example, users who are put into a virtual storage space might have much shorter timeout thresholds than users who log in from an organization-managed machine.

The following is an example of an endpoint security policy that is based on the access control policy described in the previous section. The access control policy is based on a user's host meeting one of three conditions: organization-managed host, any host, or correct IP address and time:

- **Organization-managed host.** An organization-managed host has a firewall, antivirus software, and a registry key indicating that it is managed by the organization.

- **Any host.** If users are not using their organization-managed hosts to access resources, they can still use *any host*, but with more restricted access. The only requirement for the *any host* condition is that if it is running a Windows operating system, it is using one or more specific versions of Windows, with each specific version using the most current set of updates.

- **Correct IP address and time.** Business partners can only access their assigned resources from specified IP addresses on Monday to Friday between 9 a.m. and 5 p.m. Eastern time.

The endpoint security policy is based on the access control policy and elaborates on host integrity checking and the post-login process:

- An organization-managed host must be currently running a firewall. Also, for specific versions of Windows, if there is no firewall running then the built-in Windows Firewall will automatically be enabled. An antivirus software program certified by the organization must be currently running and use a signature database that is out of date by no more than one week. The registry key is installed by the organization's information technology (IT) group either when the host is first configured or afterward by user request. Users are permitted to keep all cookies, Web browser cache entries, and downloaded files and attachments. Desktop search tools are automatically disabled at login.

- If a host is not determined to be organization-managed, it is still permitted to access the SSL VPN but must run one or more specific versions of Windows, with each specific version using the most current set of updates. After login, a user's session is established in a virtual storage space so that all data stored during the session can be erased afterward. Desktop search tools are automatically disabled at login.

- Business partners do not need to run any firewall or antivirus software, and access is based on the client host's IP address and the current time of day. Although users' sessions are not put into the virtual storage space, all browser-related data is erased after the user logs out. Downloaded files or attachments are not erased. Desktop search tools are automatically disabled at login.

If an organization has an endpoint security policy, it should deploy SSL VPN devices that can support those policies. This is especially important because endpoint security controls vary widely by device and vendor. As with authentication, each organization should conduct testing during its evaluation process to determine the endpoint security capabilities of each device being considered.

4.3.3 Select the Authentication Methods

After the organization determines how resources are to be accessed and how access control and endpoint security are to be enforced, the next step is to decide on an authentication scheme for clients. The organization should choose a scheme consistent with its security policy. For example, if two-factor authentication is already required in the enterprise, then it should also be used for SSL VPN client authentication[15]. The flexible nature of SSL VPNs, however, may require further elaboration in policy. Authentication based on digital certificates requires each host to have a certificate installed, so the organization will have to decide what type of access to permit from hosts that do not have certificates, such as hosts owned by employees or public computers. An organization might not want to allow its certificates to be installed or used on hosts that are not managed by the organization. In the case of public computers, even certificates that are stored on an external device may not work, since many public computers have their USB ports blocked to prevent the unauthorized installation of malware.

Existing external authentication infrastructures should also be leveraged if feasible. Many SSL VPN products support LDAP, RADIUS, and Active Directory, so they can be configured to access authentication servers using any of these options. The authentication server can provide group information for authenticated users, such as whether a user belongs to the Sales or Executives group, so the SSL VPN device can enforce the organization's access control policy.

SSL VPN authentication methods may be applied on an individual or group basis. This feature enables an organization to choose one form of authentication for one group, such as the Employees group, and another form of authentication for another group, such as the Executives group. The organization may also choose to base the authentication method on the specific resources, with some resources requiring stronger authentication than others.

Table 4-2 illustrates sample authentication methods for the resources defined in the previous example. Because access to the executive file share, sales database, and network infrastructure is considered to be especially sensitive, it requires two-factor authentication where the user must also use a physical token to be authenticated to the resource.

---

[15] For government agencies, OMB M-07-16 requires two-factor authentication for all remote access. It can be found at http://www.whitehouse.gov/omb/memoranda/fy2007/m07-16.pdf.

Table 4-2. Sample Authentication Methods Table

Resource	Group	Condition	Authentication
Corporate applications	Employees	Organization-managed host	RADIUS (password)
Web applications	Employees	Any host	RADIUS (password)
Executive file share	Executives	Organization-managed host	RADIUS (password and token)
Sales database	Sales	Organization-managed host	RADIUS (password and token)
Sales file share	Sales	Any host	RADIUS (password)
Extranet partner server	Business Partners	Correct IP address and time	RADIUS (password)
Network infrastructure	Administrators	Organization-managed host	TACACS+ (password and token)

Various SSL VPN products can use internal databases, combine external authentication servers with an internal database stored on the SSL VPN device itself, or just use external authentication. Either the SSL VPN database or the authentication server database can contain user-specific information, such as preferences for portal settings and bookmarks for Web sites. For ease of management, user information should be stored on the external authentication server whenever possible to reduce the amount of duplicated information, which can get out of sync.

In addition to user authentication, the organization should also evaluate different server authentication options. The SSL VPN device requires an SSL server certificate so it can authenticate itself to clients. The organization can purchase a server certificate signed by a trusted certificate authority (CA), have the server certificate signed by its own CA if it already has a public key infrastructure (PKI) in place, or give the server a self-signed certificate. A user then validates the credentials of the SSL VPN device by decrypting the certificate with the issuer's public key and possibly chaining to a trust anchor such as the trusted CA. The type and issuer of the server certificate may determine whether users from other organizations can access the VPN.[16]

Because integration with authentication servers is an area where SSL VPN products vary greatly, an organization should ensure that whatever product it chooses is able to support its authentication requirements. Any potential products should also be tested with the existing authentication servers to verify interoperability.

4.3.4 Design the Architecture

The architecture of the SSL VPN implementation refers to the selection of devices and software to provide SSL VPN services and the placement of SSL VPN devices within the existing network infrastructure. This section focuses on specific recommendations such as selection of hardware configuration, device placement and firewall configuration, routing policy and other network considerations, high availability or load balancing support, device management, client software selection, and portal design.

4.3.4.1 Selection of Hardware Configuration

A key decision to be made for the SSL VPN implementation is the type of hardware configuration to use for the SSL VPN device. There are three main types of hardware configuration: a hardware appliance, an upgrade to an existing security product, and a software solution.

---

[16] More information about server certificates and their use and management can be found in NIST SP 800-44 Version 2, *Guidelines on Securing Public Web Servers* at http://csrc.nist.gov/publications/nistpubs/.

- A hardware appliance is a device running the SSL VPN software that has been hardened by the SSL VPN device vendor to make it more secure. For example, unnecessary services and programs have been removed from the operating system, and various default settings have been changed. The hardware appliance is the most common type of SSL VPN device on the market today. Some SSL VPN appliances have accelerator options that offload SSL processing so the appliance can process more user requests. These accelerators are either external devices or cards that are installed in the SSL VPN appliance. An organization with high performance requirements should consider these options.

- Some existing security products such as firewalls or IPsec VPN gateways can be upgraded to support SSL VPNs. This option is made available by the vendor as either a software upgrade or a hardware module that is installed into the existing security device.

- A software solution is software that is installed on standard hardware, such as a server built by the organization. The hardware can either be used to support a dedicated SSL VPN service or to support other services such as a firewall or IPsec VPN.

4.3.4.2 Device Placement and Firewall Configuration

Device placement of the SSL VPN hardware is often a challenging task because the placement has security, functionality, and performance implications. It may also have an effect on other network devices such as firewalls, routers, and switches. Incorporating an SSL VPN device into a network architecture requires strong overall knowledge of network and security policy.

It is important to understand that the cryptographic protection of the SSL VPN only extends from client machines to the SSL VPN device. After the device receives the traffic from users, it is decrypted and forwarded in its original form to the destination. So if client traffic is originally sent in plaintext before it is encrypted with SSL, it is sent in plaintext from the VPN device to its destination. The SSL VPN device preserves most of the fields in the packet headers, with the exception of the source IP address and source TCP or UDP port.

There are three main options for SSL VPN device placement: as part of the organization's firewall, within the internal network, or within a demilitarized zone (DMZ). Placing the SSL VPN device outside the organization's firewalls is not recommended because the device itself receives no protection from the firewall.

Enabling VPN functionality on the firewall. This design integrates the firewall and SSL VPN device. The most common scenario is for an existing firewall product to be upgraded so it supports SSL VPNs. This option is made available by the vendor as either a software upgrade or hardware add-on. TCP port 443 for the firewall's external address must be opened on the firewall to permit users to initiate SSL VPN connections. The firewall/SSL VPN device then communicates directly with internal hosts. Figure 4-1 illustrates this design.

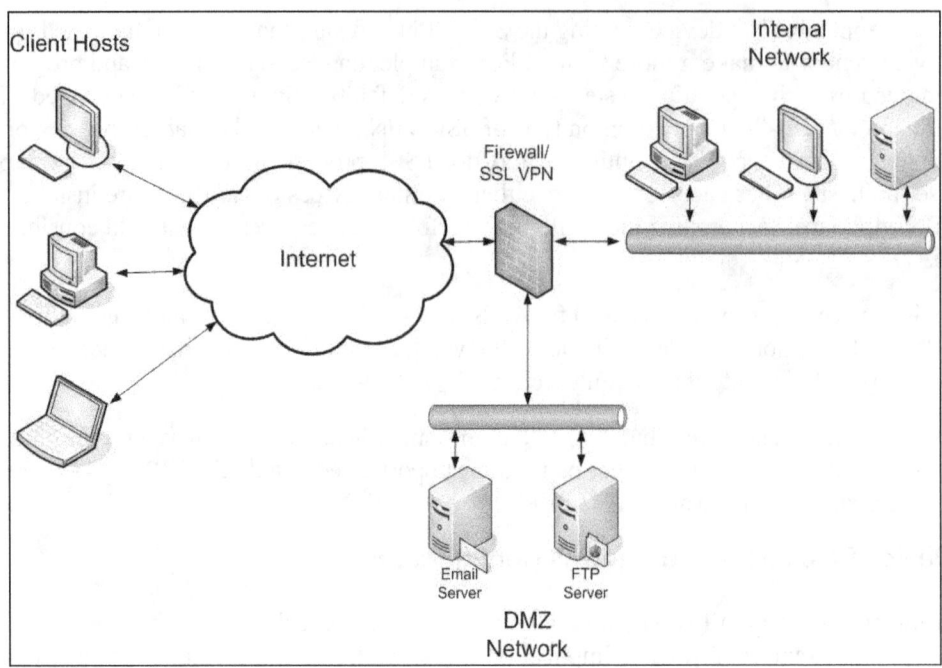

Figure 4-1. Firewall with SSL VPN Functionality

This approach has some advantages and disadvantages when compared to the other options:

Advantages:

- Holes do not need to be opened in the firewall between an external SSL VPN device and the internal network.

- Traffic between the device and the internal network must go through the firewall, so the traffic is still subject to the firewall's policies.

- Network design and system administration are simpler because there are no additional devices to administer.

Disadvantages:

- The organization is limited to the VPN functionality offered by its firewall vendor. It does not have the option of using a VPN appliance because appliances are separate hardware devices.

- The firewall is directly accessible by external users on TCP port 443. This increases the likelihood of a vulnerability on the firewall that can be exploited via these ports.

- The firewall must be augmented by SSL VPN functionality. This additional code could introduce potential vulnerabilities to the firewall.

Placing the VPN device in the internal network. This option places the VPN device entirely within the internal network behind the firewall. TCP port 443 for the address of the SSL VPN must be opened in the firewall to access the device. Figure 4-2 illustrates this design. Although it is not shown in the diagram, placement of an additional firewall between the SSL VPN device and the rest of the internal network is highly recommended. That ensures both front-end and back-end protection for the SSL VPN device.

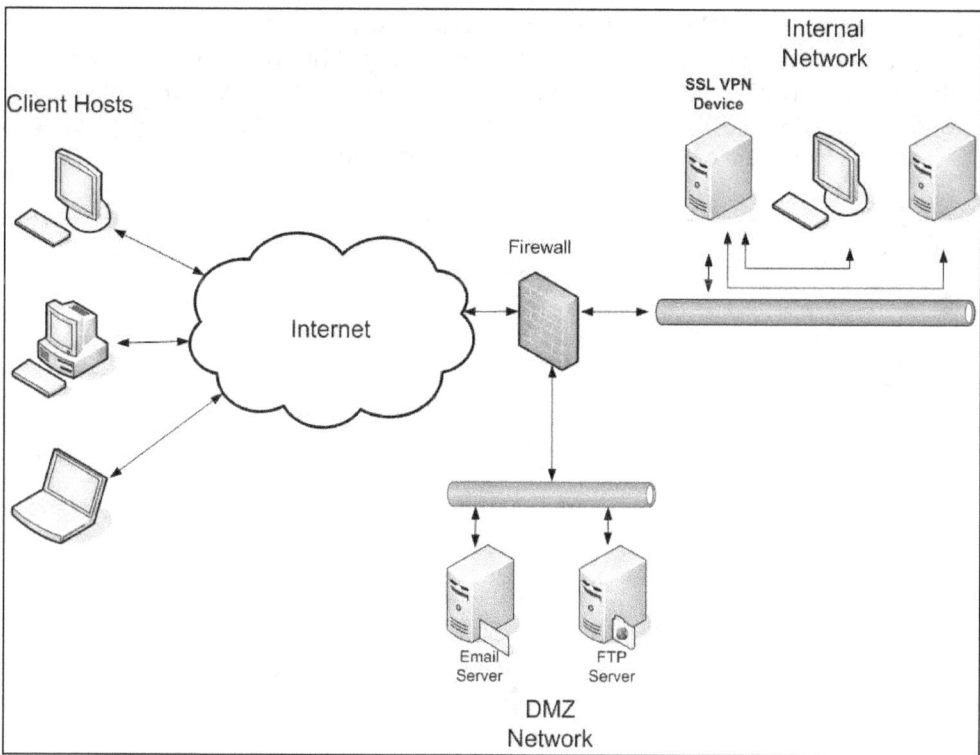

Figure 4-2. SSL VPN Device in Internal Network

Here are the advantages and disadvantages as compared with the other options:

Advantages:

- Only a single rule for a single address needs to be added to the firewall.

- The device is internal, so holes between the device and internal hosts do not have to be opened in the firewall.

- Traffic between the device and the internal network is behind the firewall, so it is protected from sniffing or Address Resolution Protocol (ARP) attacks by machines in the DMZ.

Disadvantages:

- VPN traffic bypasses the firewall entirely because all applications are tunneled through the SSL connection. This means that the firewall offers no protection from malicious traffic sent through the VPN. Instead, the VPN device must provide this protection by means of a packet filter or other methods.

- Unsolicited traffic can now be sent from the outside into the internal network (namely, to the SSL VPN device). This behavior is a violation of some corporate security policies.

- If the SSL VPN device is compromised, the attacker could have access to the internal network. This is, of course, also true if the firewall itself is compromised.

Placing the VPN device within the DMZ. This design protects traffic between the device and internal hosts as well as the device itself from external attacks. The only port that must be opened in the firewall to access the device is TCP port 443 (https). Figure 4-3 illustrates an example of a network design where the VPN device is placed in the DMZ. The DMZ is a network segment attached to a firewall interface. Although it is not shown in the diagram, placement of an additional firewall between the SSL VPN device and the internal network is highly recommended. That ensures both front-end and back-end protection for the SSL VPN device. An alternate approach is a two-DMZ architecture, placing the SSL VPN device, front- and back-ended by a firewall, on a separate DMZ segment.

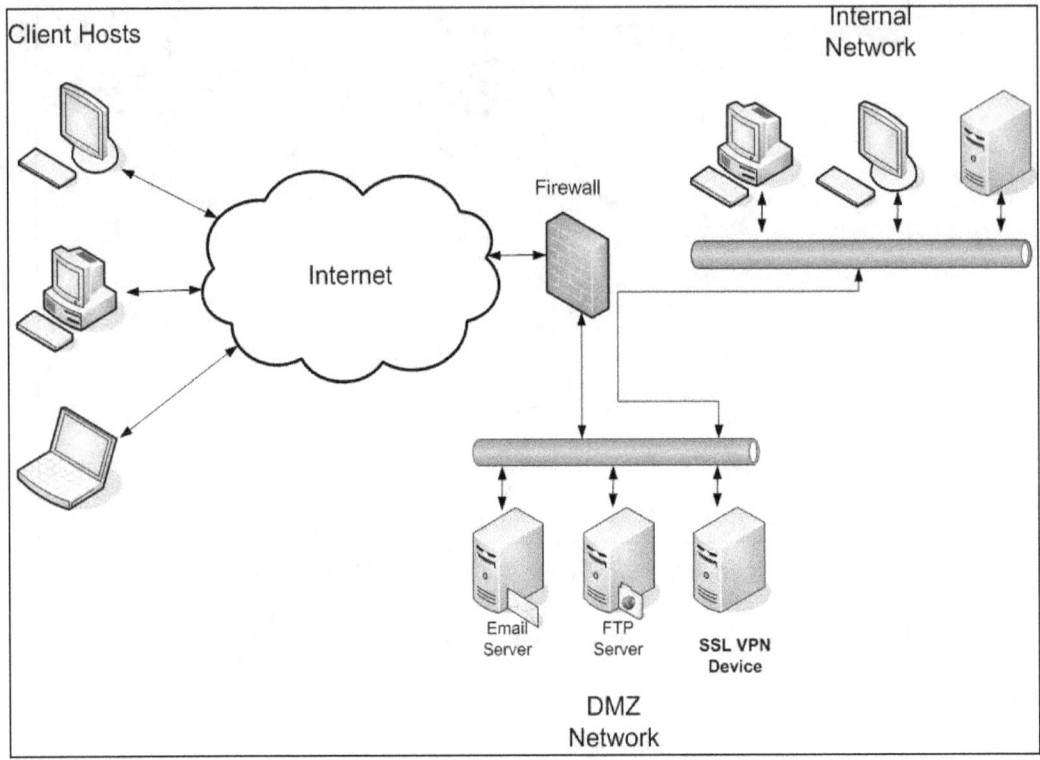

Figure 4-3. SSL VPN Device in DMZ Network

This approach has some advantages and disadvantages when compared to the other options:

Advantages:

- Compromise of the device does not necessarily mean that the attacker has full access to the internal network.

- Traffic between the device and the internal network must go through the firewall, so the traffic is still subject to the firewall's policies.

- An intrusion detection system (IDS) within the DMZ can analyze the traffic destined for the internal network for malicious activity.

Disadvantages:

- Numerous ports from the device to internal hosts must be opened in the firewall. User traffic from the VPN device will only reach internal hosts if these holes are opened. Despite one of the previously mentioned advantages of this approach, an attacker that compromises the VPN device will have access to the internal network through these holes. However, of the three solutions, this approach best minimizes the impact of a VPN breach.

- Decrypted traffic from the device to the internal network must be sent in cleartext through the DMZ network. This traffic is vulnerable to sniffing or ARP attacks by other machines in the DMZ that could be compromised by attackers.

- The firewall is bypassed when user traffic is destined for hosts in the DMZ. This assumes that clients use the VPN device to reach these DMZ hosts and do not use a split tunnel configuration (described in the next section).

It is recommended that if the VPN device is placed in the DMZ then it should be configured with two interfaces. Remote users use the external interface to connect to the device, while traffic destined for the internal network traverses the internal interface. This internal interface is connected to either another firewall or another interface on the same firewall. Figure 4-4 illustrates this design.

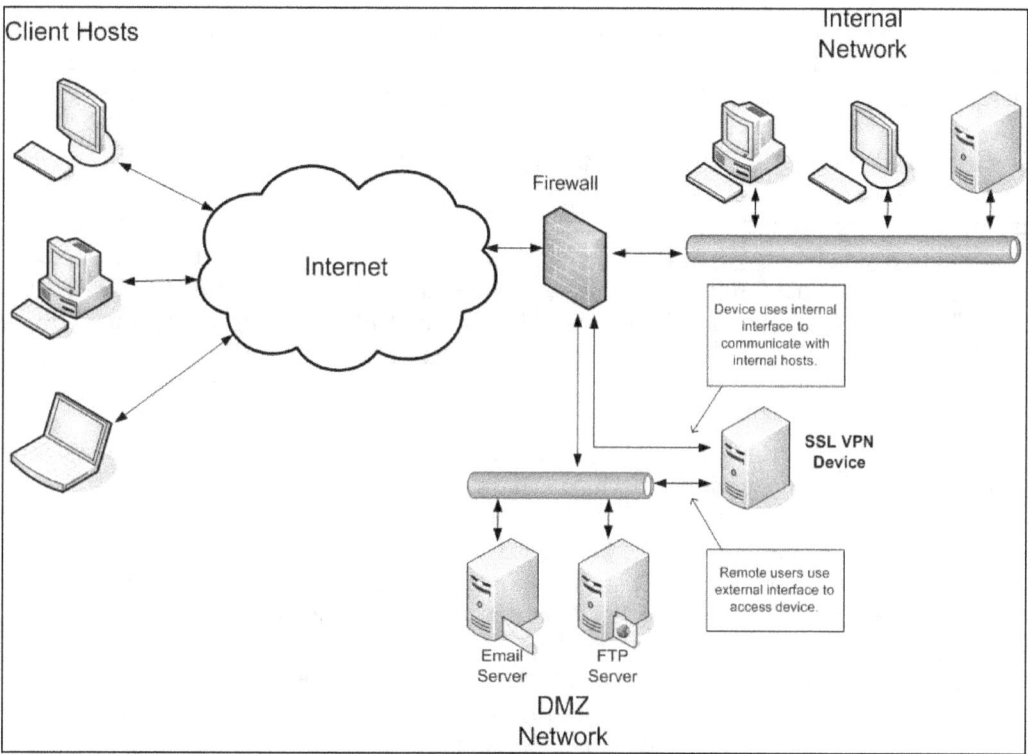

Figure 4-4. SSL VPN Device with Two Interfaces

This approach has the following advantages and disadvantages compared to the other options:

Advantages:

- All of the previously mentioned advantages of placing the device in the DMZ still apply.

- The unencrypted traffic headed for internal hosts is protected from sniffing or ARP attacks from other hosts in the DMZ.

- Only the firewall interface connected to the device's internal interface must be configured to permit traffic from the VPN device. An intruder who compromises another host in the DMZ cannot use this internal interface to access the internal network unless the VPN device is compromised too.

Disadvantages:

- Holes need to be opened in the firewall between the SSL VPN device and internal hosts.

- The firewall is bypassed when split tunneling is not used and user traffic is destined for hosts in the DMZ. Possible solutions include turning on split tunneling, putting a firewall between DMZ hosts and the VPN device, and configuring packet filtering on a router connecting the DMZ hosts to the VPN device.

- Using a second interface on the VPN device may introduce additional routing complexity (see next section).

If the organization decides to place the VPN device within the DMZ, it must decide how many holes to open in its firewall between the device and the internal network. If the organization must support many services through the SSL VPN then it may decide to completely open up all connectivity between the VPN device and the internal network. This enables VPN users to access any machine and port internally. The benefits of such an approach will have to be weighed against the costs of potential security issues.

4.3.4.3 Routing Policy and Other Network Considerations

Routing policy is as important as firewall configuration. Packets must be routed correctly within the internal network for the VPN to function properly. When the VPN components of proxying and application translation are used, routing is fairly straightforward. Packets from the VPN device that are destined for the internal network have the source address of the VPN device itself. As long as the VPN device's source address is routable in the internal network, packets will be correctly routed from internal hosts back to the VPN device.

If network extension is used, routing becomes more complicated. Network extension creates a point-to-point tunnel interface between the client machine and the VPN device. Each end of the tunnel is assigned a virtual IP address. The client's virtual IP address is used as the source address of VPN packets from the client machine. Even after traffic from the client machine reaches the VPN device and is taken out of the SSL tunnel, the source address remains the same. This means that internal hosts must know how to route the client's virtual IP address back to the VPN device, or routing will not work correctly.

For example, a client establishes a VPN connection using network extension. It receives the address of 192.168.1.200. The VPN device receives 192.168.1.1 for its virtual tunnel interface. When the VPN device forwards packets from the client to internal hosts, these internal hosts will receive packets with a source address of 192.168.1.200. If the internal routers cannot route these packets back to the VPN device, then the client will not be able to communicate with any internal hosts.

Another option is to use Network Address Translation (NAT) for clients using network extension. If NAT is used, then all packets forwarded from the VPN device to the internal network are given the source address of the VPN device. The routing configuration can therefore remain unchanged because it is assumed that internal hosts can already route traffic to the VPN device. This approach has its own disadvantages. The biggest one is that it is no longer possible to track the network activity of VPN clients by IP address because all of them share a single address. For this reason it is recommended that NAT not be used for clients using network extension.

One more issue with network extension that must be addressed is split tunneling. *Split tunneling* is defined as the process of allowing a remote VPN user to access a public network, most commonly the Internet, at the same time that the user is allowed to access resources on the VPN. A client machine that establishes a split tunnel connection with the VPN device does not send all of its network traffic through the VPN tunnel. It sends all traffic not destined for the internal (protected) network through its standard network connection and only sends traffic destined for the internal network through the VPN tunnel. Split tunneling offers the advantages of efficiency and bandwidth conservation, as traffic destined for the Internet does not have to be sent first to the VPN device. On the other hand, split tunneling also creates a potential security vulnerability. If an attacker from the Internet compromises the client machine, then this attacker can use the split tunnel to also access the organization's internal network. The organization must weigh the advantages and disadvantages of split tunneling before deciding to implement it.

If split tunneling is implemented, then the organization must decide which IP addresses will be routed through the split tunnel. If all of an organization's IP addresses are assigned to internal hosts, then the routing is straightforward, but some hosts may be in the DMZ and therefore publicly accessible. Traffic destined for these DMZ hosts will bypass the firewall if split tunneling is not used. It may therefore be more secure and efficient for the client to reach hosts located in the DMZ via the Internet rather than to use the split tunnel. If this is the case, then the organization must take care to configure the split tunnel with internal subnets only.

Section 4.3.4.2 recommends that a VPN device placed into the DMZ be configured with at least two interfaces: one for external traffic and one for internal traffic. However, using two interfaces introduces more routing complexity. The device needs to be configured with static routes that correctly point toward internal hosts or hosts in the DMZ. The routing tables for routers within the DMZ must also be configured to route all traffic destined for both interfaces on the device toward the device's external interface. If any traffic is routed toward the device's internal interface, this traffic may get dropped because it must traverse a firewall to reach the internal interface. This firewall will have no knowledge of the traffic because the original traffic from the VPN device to the DMZ hosts traversed the device's external interface and therefore did not go through the firewall. Figure 4-5 illustrates a scenario where traffic will get dropped if the packets are not correctly routed to the right interface.

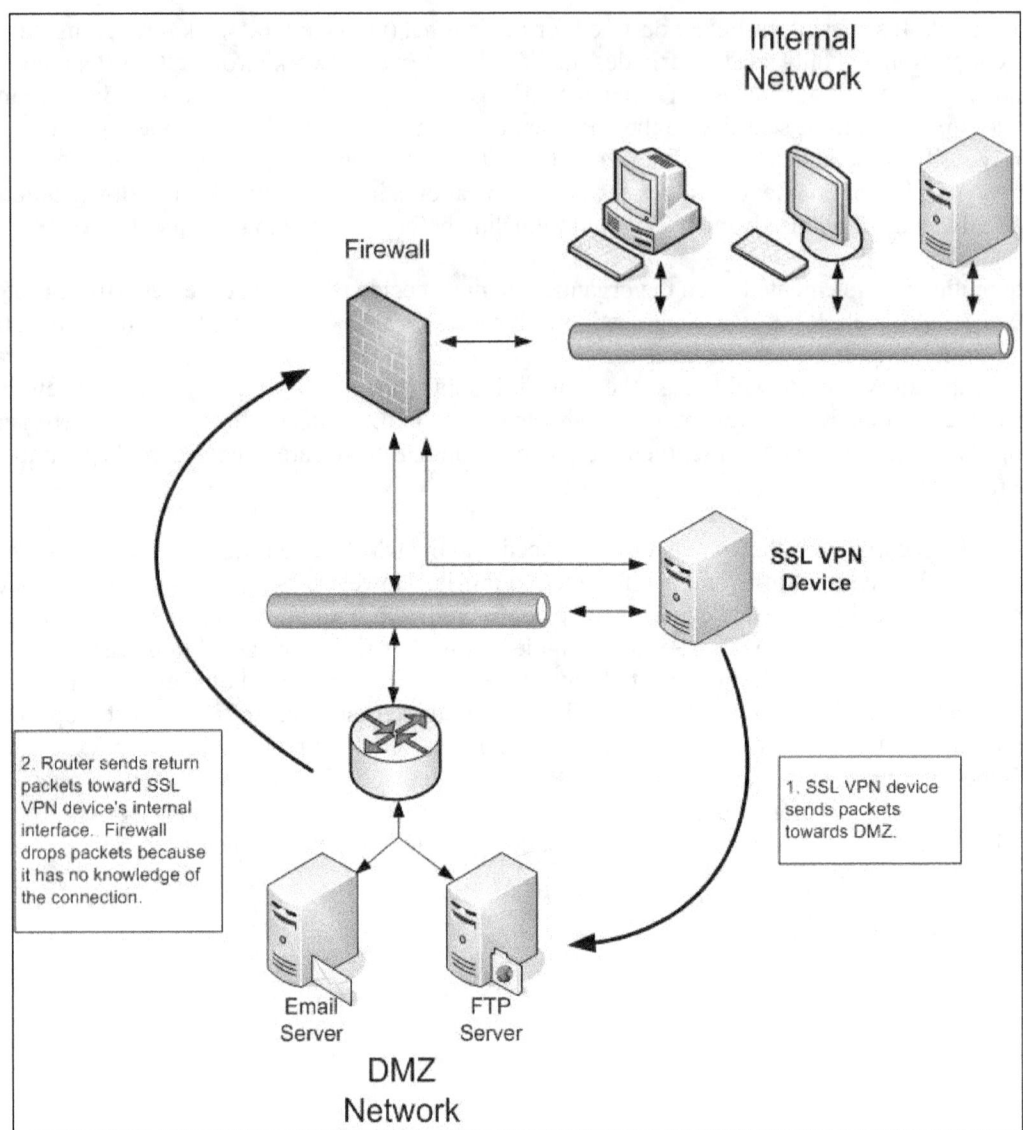

Figure 4-5. Routing Problem with SSL VPN Traffic

One final consideration for overall network policy is the issue of multiple sites. If the organization wants multiple sites to support SSL VPN services, then it must decide how to configure authentication and routing. There are several possibilities:

- Each site has an SSL VPN device, but users can only authenticate to the device at their local site. If there is a network between sites, then users can use the SSL VPN to access those other sites.

- Users can authenticate to a device at any of the sites but not simultaneously. So if there are two sites, Site A and Site B, users cannot establish VPN connections to Site A and Site B at the same time. All internal traffic must go to either Site A or Site B. Once users are authenticated, their traffic is sent to a single site and then traverses the internal network if necessary to access the other sites. This configuration could be used for backup purposes, so that a user who normally establishes a VPN connection to Site A can create a Site B VPN if the Site A VPN architecture is inaccessible.

- Users can authenticate to all sites simultaneously. Each user's routing table is configured so that packets destined for a specific site's addresses will take that site's VPN connection. If a user creates VPNs to Sites A and B simultaneously, then packets destined for a Site A subnet traverse the VPN to Site A, with the same applying to packets destined for a Site B subnet.

Note that the routing issues mentioned earlier in this section are also relevant for an architecture with multiple sites. Each site must be sure to correctly route and to not block VPN packets with addresses assigned at other sites. If the VPN devices have multiple interfaces, the packets destined for the external interface may have to be routed differently from packets destined for the internal interface. This depends on how the internal connectivity between sites is configured.

4.3.4.4 High Availability or Load Balancing Support

An organization may decide to implement high availability or load balancing. High availability may be required so the organization can meet service level agreements (SLA) for guaranteed uptime, or load balancing may be required to support a large number of users. SSL VPN products vary widely in how they support high availability and load balancing. For this reason, an organization with a need for high availability or load balancing should answer at least these questions about each device under evaluation, with testing possibly being required to receive detailed answers.

- Does the device employ an active/passive or an active/active mode architecture? An active/passive architecture only supports one active device at a time, while an active/active architecture supports two devices simultaneously. Active/passive systems are much easier to design and are therefore usually less expensive than active/active systems. Active/active systems are mostly useful in architectures where a very high load is expected, so more than one device needs to be active under normal circumstances.

- How is state information maintained across devices in a failure scenario? How long does the failover process take for proxying, translation, and network extension?

- In an active/active mode architecture, is state information for all sessions mirrored across all devices so a device failure will not disrupt any user sessions? Or does each device track state information (such as user authentication status) only for its own sessions so a device failure may require re-authentication?

- If an external load balancing solution is used, how is state information maintained throughout the architecture?

Configuration and upgrading pose additional issues. Some devices mirror configuration settings across devices, so only the active devices should be configured. Any altered settings on the passive devices will quickly be overwritten by the active device's settings. If configuration settings are not mirrored, all devices should be configured with identical settings at the same time.

For upgrades, the vendor's instructions for upgrading should be followed. Some vendors require the passive device in an active/passive mode architecture to be upgraded first. After this upgrade is complete, the newly upgraded device becomes active and the newly passive device can then be upgraded. Other vendors require the active device to be upgraded first. The active device is still handling VPN traffic while it is being upgraded and only fails over to the passive device when it is ready to reboot with the new upgrade in place. Upgrading the active device first avoids a scenario where the passive device is being upgraded and receives mirrored configuration changes from the active device in the middle of the upgrade process.

4.3.4.5 Management

The organization should design a management policy to determine who will manage the SSL VPN device and by what means. Some devices offer a partitioned or delegated management feature that allows different aspects of the device to be managed by different groups or individuals. For example, a group that manages IT for the sales department can control access control and endpoint security policies for sales resources only. System administrators can manage endpoint security regarding the type and number of patches that each client machine must have installed.

If multiple interfaces on the SSL VPN device are used, the management policy should also specify which interface permits administrative access. Some devices provide flexibility in selectively enabling administrative access on each interface, as well as permitting this access only from specific IP addresses. Various forms of authentication for administrative access may also be supported, such as smart cards and two-factor authentication. If the organization is using multiple interfaces, administrative access is commonly only configured on the interface connected to the internal network for security reasons (although allowing management from the external interface over an SSL-protected tunnel is also considered secure). If administrative access is permitted on the external interface, a stronger form of authentication than username and password should be used.

The management policy should also discuss the means of backing up and restoring the device configuration. The specific procedures will vary by device but will include a means of transferring the configuration to another computer for archiving, and of retrieving this configuration. Some devices also support the ability to create a complete image of the operating system and configuration. This feature is useful for restoring every aspect of the device's functionality at a specific point in time.

4.3.4.6 Client Software Selection

Although SSL VPNs are described as clientless, some forms of SSL VPN access such as network extension require dynamically downloaded agents to be run on the host. Even before login, the client machine may have to execute a dynamically downloaded agent that performs host integrity checks. The organization will have to ensure that these agents can run on client machines if the agents are required by access control and endpoint security policies. Once logged in, users can use common Web browsers to use the SSL VPN via proxy, but network extension requires particular browsers or versions of those browsers because they require other downloadable agents that establish the virtual network connection. If some systems such as public kiosks cannot download and execute these dynamically downloadable agents, then the organization will have to make a decision about the level of access to offer to these machines. Many SSL portal VPNs will work from all common Web browsers, but many SSL tunnel VPNs require particular browsers, and particular versions of those browsers.

4.3.4.7 Portal Design

The organization should provide a portal for users so they can login to the SSL VPN and gain access to internal resources. The portal can either be supplied by the SSL VPN device vendor or developed by the organization itself. If the organization chooses to use the portal supplied by the SSL VPN device vendor, it can customize it to match the appearance of the organization's intranet.

Portal customization features vary widely by device, but the organization should be able to alter graphics, colors, and possibly icons and the layout of the portal. The functionality of the portal will depend on the type of access to the SSL VPN. For example, resources that rely on proxying and application translation will require some sort of icon or hyperlink in the portal so users can access them. Access via network extension also requires a hyperlink or icon on the portal to initiate the network extension process. Once this takes place, however, the portal is not required to access resources because the client machine has direct access to these resources via the network extension. An organization's access control policy could determine the hyperlinks or icons that are displayed in the portal. For example, if the access control policy prohibits a user from using network extension, then the hyperlink or icon enabling network extension should not be displayed. Figure 4-6 depicts an example of a generic SSL VPN portal interface.

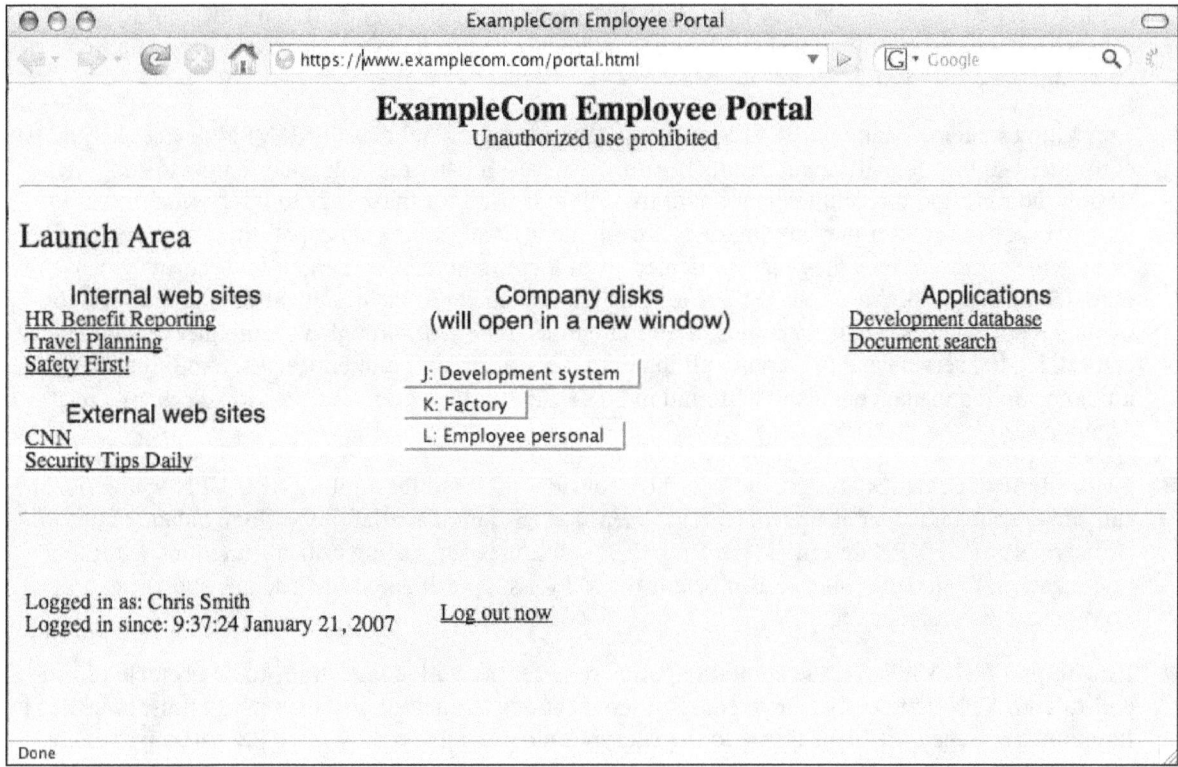

Figure 4-6. Example Portal Interface

4.3.5 Cryptography Policy and FIPS Compliance

The organization should choose a cryptography policy that fits its needs and is compliant with its requirements. In addition, Federal agencies must use only cryptographic modules whose algorithms and methods are compliant with the FIPS 140-2 specification. This topic is discussed in detail in Section 4.2.

4.3.6 Other Design Decisions

In addition to what has already been discussed in this section, there are other possible design considerations. The following items describe issues not addressed earlier:

- **IPv6.** The Office of Management and Budget (OMB) has mandated that all Federal government agencies must migrate their network backbones to support Internet Protocol version 6 (IPv6) by June 2008.[17] If the organization is planning a migration to IPv6 in the near future for compliance with this mandate or for any other reason, it should deploy an SSL VPN solution that is compliant with IPv6. There is currently no official definition of "IPv6 compliance" from a Federal government

---

[17] The OMB issued a memo titled *Transition Planning for Internet Protocol Version 6 (IPv6)* on August 2, 2005 that lays out a transition process for federal government agencies to IPv6. The memo is available at http://www.whitehouse.gov/omb/memoranda/fy2005/m05-22.pdf.

perspective.[18] It is therefore important to verify the specific functionality of an IPv6-compliant SSL VPN device as well as of all Web browsers that will connect to the SSL VPN. For example, an organization should verify if the SSL VPN device can serve as a reverse proxy for IPv6 applications and assign IPv6 addresses to network extension clients, or if it just passes IPv6 packets through.

- **Incident Response.** Organizations should consider how SSL VPN components may be affected by security-related incidents and create a design that supports effective and efficient incident response activities. For example, if an SSL VPN user's system is compromised, this should necessitate disabling the user's SSL VPN account.

- **Log Management.** Many organizations have security logging policies. SSL VPN devices should be configured so they log sufficient details regarding successful and failed login attempts to support troubleshooting and incident response activities. It is helpful for these logs to track which users log in, what type of browser they are logging in from, their IP address, what capabilities of the SSL VPN service they use, and why they may be denied from logging in (e.g., fail endpoint security because of outdated antivirus software). SSL VPN logging should adhere to the organization's policies on log management, such as requiring copies of all log entries to be sent through a secure mechanism to centralized log servers and preserving all log entries for a certain number of days. Additional guidance on log management can be found in NIST SP 800-92, *Guide to Computer Security Log Management*.[19]

- **Redundancy.** Organizations should carefully consider the need for a robust SSL VPN solution that can survive the failure of one or more components, even if high availability or load balancing is already part of the VPN design. If the SSL VPN solution is supporting critical functions within the organization, redundancy should also be considered for supporting systems such as authentication servers and directory servers.

- **End-to-end SSL VPNs.** If the corporate policy requires network connections to be protected from end-to-end, VPN devices that can create SSL connections to internal hosts via proxy must have this functionality turned off. This is due to the encryption being removed by the VPN gateway, which breaks the end-to-end requirement even if the same gateway re-encrypts the connection to the endpoint.

4.3.7 Summary of Design Decisions

Table 4-3 provides a checklist that summarizes the major design decisions made during the first two phases of the SSL VPN planning and implementation process.

Table 4-3. Design Decisions Checklist

Completed	Design Decision
Identify Requirements	
	Determine the resources to be made accessible by SSL VPN.
	Determine who must access the resources.
	Identify other current and future VPN-related requirements.
	Consider the possible technical solutions and select the one that best meets the identified requirements.

---

[18] *Federal Government Transition Internet Protocol Version 4 (IPv4) to Internet Protocol Version 6 (IPv6) Frequently Asked Questions*, February 15, 2006, http://www.whitehouse.gov/omb/egov/documents/IPv6_FAQs.pdf.

[19] For more information see NIST SP 800-92, *Guide to Computer Security Log Management*, at http://csrc.nist.gov/publications/nistpubs.

Completed	Design Decision
Design the Solution–Authentication	
	Decide which authentication methods should be supported.
Design the Solution–Access Control	
	Specify the resources to be made accessible.
	Specify the groups that have access to the resources.
	Identify the conditions under which the groups have access.
	Decide on the type of SSL VPN access to grant to users for each resource.
Design the Solution–Architecture	
	Determine where SSL VPN devices should be located within the network architecture.
	Decide on routing policy including the use of NAT and split tunneling.
	Define architecture for high availability and/or load balancing.
	Determine management policies regarding who has administrative access, for what functions, to which interfaces, and by which authentication methods.
	Verify that dynamically downloadable agents will run on client machines.
	Customize vendor-supplied portal or develop internal portal with Application Programming Interface (API) hooks.
Design the Solution–Endpoint Security	
	Define the host integrity checks that work in conjunction with access control policy.
	Decide which protection mechanisms (cache cleaner, virtual storage space, etc.) to use to protect data.
	Define timeout thresholds for inactivity and re-authentication.
Design the Solution–Cryptography	
	Choose encryption and integrity protection algorithms and key lengths.
Design the Solution–Other Design Considerations	
	Determine if IPv6 compliance is a requirement.
	Adjust incident response policy to include SSL VPN users.
	Define log management policy for SSL VPN devices.
	Consider redundancy for supporting systems (authentication or directory servers, etc.)

4.4 Implement and Test Prototype

After the SSL VPN solution has been designed, the next step is to implement and test a prototype of the design. This could be done in one or more environments, including a laboratory network, a test network, and a production network. Ideally, implementation and testing should first be performed with a laboratory network, then a test network. Only implementations in final testing should be placed onto a production network. Aspects of the solution to evaluate include the following:

- **Connectivity.** Users should be able to establish and maintain SSL VPN connections to access all resources that are intended to be accessible by the SSL VPN. It is important to verify that all of the intended applications are accessible by the operating systems and browsers that are most likely to be used by end users. Intermediate devices in the network such as routers and firewalls should not block SSL VPN connectivity, especially if the VPN device supports multiple interfaces or if multiple sites offer SSL VPN access.

- **Authentication.** Users and groups should be able to authenticate and be granted access to resources. If various groups or access to different resources require different authentication methods, then this should be verified too.

- **Access Control.** Resources should be protected in accordance with the access control policy that was established. This should be verified by monitoring network traffic and checking SSL VPN device logs. If packet filtering or multiple routing tables are used as a means of enforcing access control, then this needs to be verified as well.

- **Application and Client Interoperability.** The solution should not break or interfere with the use of existing software applications. This is especially relevant for applications that are translated to be accessible by SSL VPN, or for complex Web sites that are processed by the SSL VPN reverse proxy. It also applies to SSL VPN client software issues (e.g., conflict between active content components and other parts of the client operating system).

- **Management.** Administrators should be able to configure and manage the solution effectively and securely. This includes all components such as devices, management servers, and client software. Administrators should verify that they can create backups and restore from them.

- **Network Management.** If the organization has built a network management infrastructure, this infrastructure should periodically monitor uptime and possibly performance of the SSL VPN devices. Either the devices should send Simple Network Management Protocol (SNMP) traps to indicate a warning or critical issue or the network management system should determine this through its polling process.

- **Logging.** The logging and data management functions should work properly in accordance with the organization's policies and strategies.

- **Performance.** The SSL VPN implementation should provide adequate performance during normal and peak usage. It is important to consider not only the performance of the primary SSL VPN components but also that of intermediate devices such as routers and firewalls. Encrypted traffic often consumes more processing power than unencrypted traffic, so it may cause bottlenecks. The additional resources necessitated by SSL vary widely based on several factors, including the encryption algorithm. Performance also involves the amount of time it takes to establish an SSL VPN session; this can be affected by the demands of the back-end authentication system (e.g., RADIUS, LDAP, AD) and also by the size of the keys in the server's certificate. Also, because traffic is encapsulated within an SSL connection, intermediate network devices may need to fragment packets, possibly slowing network activity. The typical solution for these types of problems is to reduce the size of the maximum transmission unit (MTU) value on the host originating the network traffic. The MTU is the maximum allowable packet size. The MTU might be able to be lowered by the network administrator so that SSL-encapsulated packets are not large enough to require fragmentation. In many cases, the best way to test the performance under load of a prototype implementation is to use simulated traffic generators on a live test network to mimic the actual characteristics of expected traffic as closely as possible. Testing should incorporate a variety of applications that will be used with the SSL VPN implementation, especially those most likely to be affected by network throughput or latency issues. Addressing performance problems generally involves upgrading or replacing hardware, using an SSL accelerator to offload SSL processing, or reducing processing demands (e.g., limiting the number of simultaneous users, limiting the amount of encrypted application traffic).

- **Portal Design and Layout.** The portal provided for SSL VPN access should be intuitive and straightforward to navigate. It should also contain the features required by users and only display the resources for which the current user is authorized. If relevant, it should be consistent with the organization's guidelines for Web sites and applications.

- **Security of the Implementation.** Parts of the SSL VPN's implementation, such as the SSL code or the firewall code, may contain vulnerabilities that attackers could exploit. Organizations with high security requirements may want to perform extensive vulnerability assessments against the SSL VPN components. At a minimum, the testers should update the SSL VPN components with the latest patches and configure the components following sound security practices. If the device supports features to protect against cross-site scripting, Structured Query Language (SQL) injection, and buffer overflow attacks, then these features should be enabled.

- **Endpoint Security.** Only the client machines that pass the security requirements (e.g., firewall, antivirus software) should be granted access to the SSL VPN. If any security mechanism such as a virtual storage space or cache cleaner is enabled during a login session, these mechanisms should erase all data downloaded during the VPN session.

- **Default Settings.** SSL VPN implementations have many default configuration settings. SSL VPN implementers should carefully review the default values for each setting and alter the settings as necessary to support their design goals. They should also ensure that the implementation does not unexpectedly "drop back" to default settings for interoperability or other reasons.

4.4.1 Application and Client Interoperability

Application and client interoperability is a key requirement for a successful SSL VPN implementation. This is especially important because of the diversity of both the accessible applications and the potential user client environments. It is difficult to predict how a specific client will interoperate with a specific application through the SSL VPN.

Some examples of potential interoperability issues are as follows:

- Complex Web applications that use JavaScript, Flash, or other languages may not function correctly after being translated by the SSL VPN proxy component. For example, these applications may include URLs to internal sites that cannot be traversed because they are not visible to the proxy. Even if the proxy can translate some of the programming code, it might not be able to translate all of it.

- Some SSL VPN devices alter the URL when they function as a proxy. In other words, the user enters a URL for a Web site to access, but this URL is altered so it no longer resembles what was originally entered. This alteration may prevent some applications from working correctly.

- Clients may not be able to download and install the active content controls that are required to establish the SSL VPN network extension. This may be due to popup blocker settings in the user's browser, managed desktop settings that prevent the installation of active content controls for security reasons, or idiosyncrasies on the client machine.

- Endpoint security mechanisms may not work correctly on a client machine, either preventing login or failing to erase sensitive data from the machine after the session is over. These issues may be due to idiosyncrasies on the client machine, a conflict with other security programs such as personal firewalls, or a conflict between multiple endpoint security programs that are running at the same time.

The best way to determine if there are interoperability issues is to test as many configurations as possible in a lab or test environment. The most popular configurations of all target operating system platforms (e.g., Windows, Mac OS X, Linux) should be tested with the most popular Web browsers (e.g., Internet Explorer, Firefox, Opera, Safari). The testing process should also attempt to verify that the organization's applications are accessible in each commonly used browser and operating system. It is impossible to test every single permutation of client environment because of the wide variety of possible configuration settings on each machine, but at least a default configuration of each commonly used operating system and browser should be tested.

Disk imaging technologies could be helpful in the interoperability testing process. Baseline images of each operating system could be created and then restored to the baseline after each iteration of testing. This practice helps to ensure consistency during the testing process and may help to identify specific configurations that result in interoperability problems. Virtual machine technology could also be helpful in a similar way, where a "snapshot" of the baseline operating system running in a virtual machine is created and restored after each testing iteration. Virtual machine technology streamlines the interoperability testing process by vastly reducing the time to restore a machine to its initial baseline condition.

If interoperability problems are discovered, the organization should work with the SSL VPN device vendor to troubleshoot them. Helping the vendor to replicate these problems is essential for this process. The problems may be solved by configuration changes, patches provided by the vendor, or modifications to the application or operating system that is causing the problem. If an interoperability problem with an application cannot be solved, the organization may have to reconsider whether it will be possible to enable remote access for the application.

4.5 Deploy the Solution

Once testing is complete and any issues have been resolved, the next phase of the SSL VPN planning and implementation model involves deploying the solution. It is important to launch a pilot program before enterprise-wide deployment. A pilot program should consist of users who will be helpful for testing the SSL VPN solution for interoperability, functionality, and usability. Pilot users should fall in a broad range of technical knowledge levels to evaluate the organization's ability to answer a wide variety of technical questions regarding the SSL VPN solution. At the same time, the limited nature of a pilot program helps to identify a set of problems that could potentially affect a greater audience, while offering the opportunity to fix these problems before the SSL VPN is used by the entire enterprise.

Part of the pilot program includes end user training and help desk support to assist users in understanding and using the SSL VPN's features. End users can either be trained in hands-on sessions or larger lectures. Users also require documentation that serves as a reference in supplementing the training. Help desk personnel should receive more detailed technical training so they can help users to troubleshoot problems and walk them through the process of establishing VPN connectivity. If the pilot program is small enough, the group deploying the SSL VPN solution may provide technical support to pilot users, with training for help desk personnel occurring later.

After the pilot program has been launched, it is recommended that the organization gradually migrate existing network infrastructure, applications, and users to the new SSL VPN solution. This phased deployment provides administrators an opportunity to evaluate the impact of the SSL VPN solution and resolve issues before enterprise-wide deployment. Most of the issues that can occur during SSL VPN deployment are the same type of issues that occur during any large IT deployment.

The organization should also produce technical documentation somewhere in the deployment phase. The documentation should include the following:

- Instructions on configuring the SSL VPN devices to their present state

- Access control policy
- Routing and firewall configuration policies
- Standard operating procedures for the SSL VPN implementation
- Endpoint security requirements.

Typical issues that could arise at various stages of the deployment process are as follows:

- Encrypted traffic can negatively affect services such as firewalls, intrusion detection, Quality of Service (QoS), remote monitoring (RMON) probes, and congestion control protocols.
- Unexpected performance issues may arise, either with the SSL VPN components themselves or with intermediate devices such as routers.
- SSL VPN traffic may not flow properly on some production networks because of firewalls, routers, or other intermediate packet filtering devices that block SSL VPN traffic.
- The environment may change during the deployment. For example, active content controls used for network extensions may be broken by a client operating system update or new application installation. This issue can be handled rather easily in a managed environment, but it can pose a major problem if users have full control over their systems and can select their own client software.

4.6 Manage the Solution

The last phase of the SSL VPN planning and implementation model lasts the longest. Managing the solution involves maintaining the SSL VPN architecture, policies, software, and other components of the deployed solution. Examples of typical maintenance actions are testing and applying patches or software updates to the SSL VPN devices, deploying SSL VPN connectivity to additional remote sites, renewing SSL server certificates that are going to expire, and adapting the policies as requirements change. It is also important to monitor the performance of SSL VPN components so that potential resource issues can be identified and addressed before performance becomes seriously degraded. Another important task is to perform testing periodically to verify that the access controls are functioning as expected. Any new hardware, software, or significant configuration changes start the process again at the Identify Requirements phase. This ensures that the SSL VPN solution lifecycle operates effectively and efficiently.

Another aspect of managing the SSL VPN solution is handling operational issues. For example, poor performance may be caused by connection problems such as fragmentation. Fragmentation occurs when network packets are broken down into smaller fragments, which then need to be reassembled at the receiving host. A network sniffer such as tcpdump or Wireshark is typically very helpful in troubleshooting SSL VPN connections. A sniffer allows the administrator to analyze the communications as they take place and correct problems. Because SSL traffic is encrypted and may not be decipherable from a standard packet capture, some SSL VPN devices provide decrypted network sniffing capability so that connectivity from one of the VPN endpoints may be analyzed. SSL VPN device logs and client logs may also be valuable resources during troubleshooting. Additionally, firewall and router logs may validate whether the SSL VPN traffic is reaching them, passing through them, or being blocked.

4.7 Summary

This section describes a phased approach to SSL VPN planning and implementation and highlights various issues that may be of significance to implementers. The following summarizes the key points from the section:

- The use of a phased approach for SSL VPN planning and implementation can help to achieve successful SSL VPN deployments. The five phases of the approach are as follows:

  1. **Identify Requirements.** Identify the requirements for remote access and determine how they can best be met.

  2. **Design the Solution.** Make design decisions in five areas: access control, endpoint security, authentication methods, architecture, and cryptography policy.

  3. **Implement and Test a Prototype.** Test a prototype of the designed solution in a lab, test, or production environment to identify any potential issues.

  4. **Deploy the Solution.** Gradually deploy the SSL VPN solution throughout the enterprise, beginning with a pilot program.

  5. **Manage the Solution.** Maintain the SSL VPN components and resolve operational issues. Repeat the planning and implementation process when significant changes need to be incorporated into the solution.

- The organization should base its access control policy on its organizational requirements for remote access. These requirements stipulate which resources should be accessed by which groups or individuals. The access control policy could provide additional requirements and make access to resources dependent on other characteristics such as the authentication method used, computer type and location, and user identification.

- The endpoint security policy specifies the host integrity checks that are performed before a host logs in. The policy also defines the checks that are performed after logout to guarantee the security of data that is downloaded during the VPN session.

- The organization should select an authentication solution that is consistent with its security policy. The method of authentication can vary by user, group, or specific resource.

- There are three main types of hardware configuration: a hardware appliance, an option to an existing security product, and a software solution. The hardware appliance configuration is the most common.

- The placement of an SSL VPN device has potential security, functionality, and performance implications.

- Routing policy is an important consideration, especially if the VPN implementation supports network extension, split tunneling, or multiple sites. It is recommended that NAT not be used so traffic to and from individual remote hosts can be tracked.

- SSL VPN devices vary widely in how they support load balancing and high availability, so the organization should select a device that supports its load balancing or high availability requirements.

- Although SSL VPNs are described as clientless, some forms of SSL VPN access such as network extension require dynamically downloaded agents to be run on the host.

- SSL VPN users require access to a portal so they can login to the SSL VPN and gain access to internal resources. The portal can either be supplied by the SSL VPN device vendor or developed by the organization itself. The organization's access control policy determines the VPN options available to a user.

- The strongest possible cryptographic algorithms and key lengths that are considered secure for current practice should be used for encryption and integrity protection unless they are incompatible with performance and export constraints. For government agencies, traffic that requires protection must employ FIPS-compliant cryptographic algorithms.

- Other design decisions include IPv6 capability, incident response, log management, and redundancy.

- Testing of the prototype implementation should evaluate multiple factors including connectivity, authentication, access control, endpoint security, application and client interoperability, management, network management, logging, performance, portal design and layout, and security.

- It is important to launch a pilot program before enterprise-wide deployment. Once this program has been launched, it is recommended to gradually migrate existing network infrastructure, applications, and users to the new SSL VPN solution.

- After implementation, the SSL VPN solution needs to be maintained. Such maintenance can include applying patches and deploying SSL VPN connectivity to additional remote sites. Operational issues also need to be addressed and resolved.

- Organizations should implement technical, operational, and management controls that support and complement SSL VPN implementations. Examples include having control over all entry and exit points for the protected networks, ensuring the security of all SSL VPN endpoints, and incorporating SSL VPN considerations into organizational policies.

5. SSL VPN Recommended Practices

This section summarizes the information presented in the previous sections as a manageable and actionable set of recommendations that organizations can implement to provide reasonable assurance that their SSL VPN solutions are providing adequate security and are themselves secured properly. To be effective, an SSL VPN should have its security considerations incorporated throughout the entire IT life cycle, involving everything from policy to operations. This section references a five-phase life cycle model to help organizations determine at what point in their SSL VPN deployments a recommended practice might be relevant. The model is based on one introduced in NIST SP 800-64, *Security Considerations in the Information System Development Life Cycle*[20]. Organizations may follow a project management methodology or life cycle model that does not directly map to the phases in the model that is presented in this section, but the types of tasks in the methodology and their sequencing are probably similar.

Table 5-1 presents the recommended practices corresponding to the life cycle phases. Each recommendation is accompanied by a brief explanation of the rationale for its inclusion and section reference for more information, and is rated as *recommended practice* or *should consider*. Organizations are strongly encouraged to adopt the *recommended practices*. Failure to implement them significantly increases the risk of an SSL VPN security failure or makes it more difficult to assess the overall security of the SSL VPN system. Organizations should also examine each of the *should consider* recommendations to determine their applicability to the target environment. In general, *should consider* measures enhance security beyond what can be achieved through the *recommended practices*. A *should consider* should be rejected only if it is infeasible or if the reduction in risk from its implementation does not justify its cost.

Table 5-1. SSL VPN Life Cycle Phase Recommendations

Life Cycle Phase	Recommendation	Rationale	Rating
Initiation	Identify which resources or services need to be available for remote access and who should be able to access them through the SSL VPN.	This will assist in creating a granular access control list. Reference: 4.1	Recommended Practice
	Consider future needs as well as current.	This will assist in choosing a scalable solution. Reference: 4.1	Should Consider
	Determine other requirements such as anticipated performance requirements (normal and peak loads), service level agreement (SLA) guarantees, and the use of multiple languages.	This will assist in choosing a comprehensive solution. Reference: 4.1	Should Consider
Acquisition/ Development	SSL VPNs should support the required algorithms for symmetric encryption, key exchange, and hash functions; and the required key lengths.	Some organizations, such as Federal agencies, have strict requirements for encryption and integrity protection. All cryptographic algorithms for Federal agencies must be FIPS-approved. Reference: 3.6	Recommended Practice

---

[20] NIST SP 800-64 can be downloaded from http://csrc.nist.gov/publications/nistpubs/.

Life Cycle Phase	Recommendation	Rationale	Rating
	Weigh the different technical solutions after the deployment requirements are identified.	It is possible that other protocols such as SSH or IPsec provide a better technical solution than SSL. This is especially pertinent if a VPN solution already exists, because it could potentially be leveraged to meet the identified requirements. Reference: 4.1	Recommended Practice
Implementation	SSL VPNs that are to be used in applications that must be FIPS-compliant must use TLS 1.0 or later for their SSL VPN systems. Further, those systems must be able to be configured to only use TLS 1.0 or later.	This configuration ensures proper compliance and security level for the organization. Reference: 4.2.1	Recommended Practice
	SSL VPNs that are to be used in applications that must be FIPS-compliant must be able to be configured to only use cipher suites with FIPS-compliant encryption.	A client that is offering a cipher suite with non-compliant encryption might use the SSL negotiation to cause the SSL VPN gateway to create an SSL session that is inappropriate for the security level of the organization. Reference: 4.2.3	Recommended Practice
	SSL VPNs that are to be used in applications that must be FIPS-compliant must be able to be configured to only use FIPS-compliant key sizes and hash functions in these certificates.	This configuration ensures proper compliance and security level for the organization. Reference: 4.2.5	Recommended Practice
	Design the access control policy by listing the resources that will be accessed through the SSL VPN, the groups or users, the conditions under which the resources should be accessible by the groups, and how the VPN should be used to access the resources.	This allows a more manageable and granular access control policy. Reference: 4.3.1	Recommended Practice
	Run host integrity checks before the login process.	This looks for malware such as keystroke loggers or viruses, validates that the operating system and applications have current patches, looks for out-of-compliance software, etc. Reference: 4.3.2	Recommended Practice
	An endpoint security policy should consider how to enforce endpoint security on a client system after the user has logged out.	This includes the use of cache cleaners and virtual storage space. Reference: 4.3.2	Should Consider

Life Cycle Phase	Recommendation	Rationale	Rating
	If a user forgets to log out, the SSL VPN device should be able to perform an automatic logout after a specific period of inactivity.	This protects against open connections that could be hijacked by attackers. Reference: 4.3.2	Should Consider
	The organization should choose an authentication scheme consistent with its security policy.	This will ensure compatibility and can leverage current authentication methods. If two-factor authentication is already required, then it should also be used for SSL VPN client authentication. Reference: 4.3.3	Recommended Practice
	Existing external authentication infrastructures should also be leveraged if feasible.	Many SSL VPN products support LDAP, RADIUS, and Active Directory, so they can be configured to access authentication servers using any of these options. Reference: 4.3.3	Recommended Practice
	In addition to user authentication, the organization should also evaluate different server authentication options.	The SSL VPN device requires an SSL server certificate so it can authenticate itself to clients. Reference: 4.3.3	Should Consider
	An organization with high performance requirements should consider a hardware SSL VPN appliance with accelerators.	Hardware accelerators offload SSL processing so the appliance can process more user requests. Reference: 4.3.4.1	Should Consider
	Place the SSL VPN device inside the organization's firewall.	Placing the SSL VPN device outside the firewall is not recommended because the traffic destined for the internal network still has to go through the firewall, limiting any value provided by the VPN. The traffic between the VPN device and internal hosts is not encrypted by SSL and potentially vulnerable to sniffing attacks. Also, the device itself receives no protection from the firewall. Reference: 4.3.4.2	Should Consider

Life Cycle Phase	Recommendation	Rationale	Rating
	It is recommended that if the VPN device is placed in the DMZ then it should be configured with two interfaces.	Remote users use the external interface to connect to the device, while traffic destined for the internal network traverses the internal interface. This internal interface is connected to either another firewall or another interface on the same firewall. Reference: 4.3.4.2	Should Consider
	It is recommended that NAT not be used for clients using network extension.	NAT makes it difficult to track the network activity of VPN clients by IP address because all of them share a single address. Additionally, client machines lose the option of offering file or print services to be shared by internal hosts. Reference: 4.3.4.3	Recommended Practice
	The organization should design a management policy to determine who will manage the SSL VPN device and by what means.	This will establish points of contact and accountability. Reference: 4.3.4.5	Recommended Practice
	If administrative access is permitted on the external interface, a stronger form of authentication should be used than username and password.	It is important to protect external interfaces that may be accessible by attackers. Reference: 4.3.4.5	Recommended Practice
	The management policy should address the means of backing up and restoring the device configuration.	Regular configuration backups should be performed as well as periodic testing of restore procedures. Reference: 4.3.4.5	Recommended Practice
	The organization should provide a portal for users so they can login to the SSL VPN and gain access to internal resources.	This is the main interface for users. Reference: 4.3.4.7	Recommended Practice
	If the organization is planning a migration to IPv6 in the near future for compliance or for any other reason, it should deploy an SSL VPN solution that is compliant with IPv6.	The Office of Management and Budget (OMB) has mandated that all Federal government agencies must migrate their network backbones to support IPv6 by June 2008. Reference: 4.3.6	Recommended Practice
	Organizations should consider how SSL VPN components may be affected by security-related incidents and create a design that supports effective and efficient incident response activities.	Creating effective and efficient incident response procedures can lessen the damage caused by attackers. Reference: 4.3.6	Recommended Practice

Life Cycle Phase	Recommendation	Rationale	Rating
	SSL VPN devices should be configured so they log sufficient details regarding successful and failed login attempts to support troubleshooting and incident response activities.	Establishing effective event logging and review procedures can lessen the damage if a security event occurs. Reference: 4.3.6	Recommended Practice
	Implement and test a prototype of the design.	Test a prototype of the designed solution in a lab, test, or production environment to identify any potential issues. Reference: 4.4	Should Consider
	Launch a pilot program before enterprise-wide deployment.	A pilot program should consist of users who will be helpful for testing the SSL VPN solution for interoperability, functionality, and usability. Reference: 4.5	Should Consider
	After the pilot program has been launched, it is recommended that the organization gradually migrate existing network infrastructure, applications, and users to the new SSL VPN solution.	This phased deployment provides administrators an opportunity to evaluate the impact of the SSL VPN solution and resolve issues before enterprise-wide deployment. Reference: 4.5	Recommended Practice
	The organization should produce technical documentation somewhere in the deployment phase.	This will assist with configuration and troubleshooting of the SSL VPN solution. Reference: 4.5	Recommended Practice
Operations/ Maintenance	Organizations should implement other measures that support and complement SSL VPN implementations.	These measures help to ensure that the SSL VPN solution is implemented in an environment with the technical, management, and operational controls necessary to provide sufficient security for the SSL VPN implementation. Reference: 4	Recommended Practice
	Perform ongoing monitoring, upgrading, and securing of the SSL VPN solution.	This includes testing and applying patches or software updates to the SSL VPN devices, deploying SSL VPN connectivity to additional remote sites, renewing SSL server certificates that are going to expire, and adapting the policies as requirements change. Reference: 4.6	Recommended Practice

Life Cycle Phase	Recommendation	Rationale	Rating
	Monitor the performance of SSL VPN components.	Potential resource issues can be identified and addressed before performance becomes seriously degraded. Reference: 4.6	Recommended Practice
	Perform testing periodically to verify that the access controls are functioning as expected.	This may reveal security weaknesses that need to be mitigated. Reference: 4.6	Recommended Practice

6. Alternatives to SSL VPNs

Although SSL VPNs are flexible enough to meet many needs, there are certain cases when other types of VPNs may provide a better solution. This section lists several VPN protocols that are used as alternatives to SSL VPNs in different scenarios. This section groups the types of VPN by the approximate layer of the TCP/IP model at which they function, because many of the protocols' characteristics are based on the layer they use. SSL is the prevalent transport layer VPN protocol; this section discusses several data link layer, network layer, and application layer VPN protocols. For each protocol, a brief description is provided, along with a description of the circumstances under which it may be more advantageous than an SSL VPN.

6.1 Data Link Layer VPN Protocols

Data link layer VPN protocols function below the network layer in the TCP/IP model. This means that various network protocols, such as IP, Internetwork Packet Exchange (IPX), and Network Basic Input/Output System (NetBIOS) Extended User Interface (NetBEUI), can usually be used with a data link layer VPN. Most VPN protocols, such as IPsec, only support IP, so data link layer VPN protocols may provide a viable option for protecting networks running non-IP protocols and for networks running more than one network protocol (such as IP and IPX at the same time).

The most commonly implemented data link layer VPN protocols are typically used on top of the Point-to-Point Protocol (PPP) and are most often used to secure modem-based connections. PPP, not the VPN protocol itself, typically provides encryption and authentication services for the traffic. The standards for PPP only reference supporting Data Encryption Standard (DES) for encryption and Password Authentication Protocol (PAP) and Challenge Handshake Authentication Protocol (CHAP) for authentication. Because there are known weaknesses in these algorithms, data link layer VPN protocols often make use of additional protocols and services to provide stronger encryption and authentication for VPN connections. The most commonly used data link layer VPN protocols are as follows:

- Point-to-Point Tunneling Protocol (PPTP) Version 2

    - PPTP provides a protected tunnel between a PPTP-enabled client (e.g., a personal computer) and a PPTP-enabled server. Each system that may use PPTP needs to have PPTP client software installed and configured appropriately.

    - PPTP uses Generic Routing Encapsulation (GRE) to transport data. Most packet filtering devices block this protocol by default, so they may need to be reconfigured to permit it in systems that use PPTP for a VPN. In addition to the GRE connection, PPTP also establishes a separate control channel using TCP port 1723.

    - Microsoft has created its own PPP encryption mechanism for use with PPTP, Microsoft Point-to-Point Encryption (MPPE); it uses a 40-bit or 128-bit key with the RSA RC4 algorithm. Microsoft has also created MS-CHAP to provide stronger authentication than PAP and CHAP; nevertheless, researchers have found serious weaknesses in MS-CHAP.[21]

    - The original version of PPTP contained serious security flaws. PPTP version 2 addressed many of these issues, but researchers have identified weaknesses with it as well (in addition to the MS-CHAP issues).

---

[21] For more information please refer to http://www.schneier.com/paper-pptpv2.pdf.

- **Layer 2 Tunneling Protocol (L2TP)**

    - Like PPTP, L2TP protects communications between an L2TP-enabled client and an L2TP-enabled server, and it requires L2TP client software to be installed and configured on each user system.

    - Unlike PPTP, which relies on GRE to tunnel data, L2TP uses its own tunneling protocol, which runs over UDP port 1701. Because of this, L2TP may be easier to pass through packet filtering devices than PPTP.

    - L2TP can support multiple sessions within the same tunnel.

    - L2TP with IPsec is an established standard of the IETF (RFC 3193).

    - In addition to the PPP-provided authentication methods, L2TP can also use other methods, such as RADIUS and Terminal Access Controller Access Control System (TACACS+).

    - L2TP often uses IPsec to provide encryption and key management services.

- **Layer 2 Forwarding (L2F)**

    - Unlike PPTP and L2TP, L2F is intended for use between network devices, such as an ISP's network access server and an organization's VPN gateway. Users establish unprotected connections from their computers to the ISP. The ISP recognizes that the users' traffic should be tunneled to the organization, so it authenticates each user and the organization's VPN gateway, and then provides protection for the traffic between the ISP and the organization. The use of L2F requires the ISP's support and participation.

    - Because L2F is not client-based, users' systems do not need L2F client software or configuration. However, this also means that communications between the users' systems and the ISP are completely unprotected.

    - Like L2TP, L2F can use authentication protocols such as RADIUS and TACACS+. L2F does not support encryption.

L2TP was intended to replace PPTP and L2F. When configured properly, L2TP combined with IPsec can provide strong encryption and authentication. PPTP should not be used to protect communications because of its known weaknesses. Because L2F can provide only limited protection for portions of communications that involve a participating ISP, L2TP should be used instead of L2F when the link from the remote user to the ISP needs to be protected (which is normally the case). L2TP with IPsec is a viable option for providing confidentiality and integrity for dial-up communications, particularly for organizations that contract VPN services to an ISP.

6.2 Network Layer VPN Protocols

Network layer VPN protocols apply to all applications and are not application-specific. This allows some or all network communications between two hosts or networks to be protected without modifying any applications. IPsec is the most common network layer security control used to create VPNs. It is a framework of open standards for ensuring private communications over public networks. IPsec protocols work together in various combinations to provide protection for communications. The primary components of IPsec include the Authentication Header (AH), Encapsulating Security Payload (ESP), Internet Key Exchange (IKE), and IP Payload Compression Protocol (IPComp).[22]

In many environments, network layer controls such as IPsec provide a much better solution than transport or application layer controls because of the difficulties in adding controls to individual applications. Another advantage of network layer controls is that since IP information (e.g., IP addresses) is added at this layer, the controls can protect both the data within the packets and the IP information for each packet. Nevertheless, network layer controls provide less control and flexibility for protecting specific applications than transport and application layer controls.

6.3 Application Layer "VPNs"

As discussed in Section 2.1, each application layer protocol provides protection for only a single application. In many cases, the protocol protects only a portion of the application data. For example, the S/MIME and OpenPGP application protocols can be used in conjunction with email servers to encrypt the body of an email, but not the email headers (which include addressing information). Doing the encrypting at the mail server creates a secure path between the mail servers, but only for the data covered by the cryptographic changes.

It is difficult to call such encryption a VPN. It is not a network: it is a set of paths. Even if the entire message is encrypted, such as with Voice over IP (VoIP) that is using encryption, it is by no means a network: it is just a collection of encrypted data. Thus, it is incorrect to call anything above the network layer a "VPN", although many companies market their application-layer encryption products as such.

A commonly used application layer protocol suite is Secure Shell (SSH), which contains secure replacements for several unencrypted application protocols, including telnet, Remote Copy Protocol (RCP), and FTP. The SSH client program itself provides protection for remote logins to another system. Some organizations extend the use of the SSH application by establishing SSH tunnels between hosts, and then passing other communications through the tunnels. This allows many applications to be protected at one time through a single tunnel. Generally, the tunnel is constructed between a remote user's system and a server within the organization that the user can log into. Because a single SSH tunnel can provide protection for one or more applications at the same time, it is technically a transport layer VPN protocol, not application layer.

SSH tunnel-based VPNs are resource-intensive to set up. They require the installation and configuration of SSH client software on each user's machine, as well as the reconfiguration of client applications to use the tunnel. Each user must also have login privileges on a server within the organization. Generally, users need to have solid technical skills so that they can configure systems and applications themselves, as well as troubleshoot problems that occur. Because of this, using SSH tunnels as a VPN is uncommon, particularly when compared to SSL VPN deployment.

6.4 Summary

Section 6 describes the main alternatives to SSL VPNs. Data link layer VPN protocols, such as PPTP, L2TP, and L2F; network layer VPN protocols, primarily IPsec; and application layer "VPN" protocols, including OpenPGP and SSH, are all effective alternatives to SSL VPNs for particular needs and environments. Table 6-1 provides a high-level comparison of the alternatives. The following summarizes the key points from Section 6:

---

[22] Detailed information on the IPsec components may be found in NIST SP 800-77, *Guide to IPsec VPNs*, available from http://csrc.nist.gov/publications/nistpubs/.

- **Data link layer VPNs** can protect various network protocols, so they are often used for non-IP protocols. Data link layer VPNs are most commonly used on top of PPP to secure modem-based connections, although PPP actually encrypts the traffic.
    - **PPTP** protects communications between a PPTP-enabled client and a PPTP-enabled server, and uses GRE to transport data between them.
    - **L2TP** protects communications between an L2TP-enabled client and an L2TP-enabled server and uses its own tunneling protocol over UDP port 1701 to transport data.
    - **L2F** protects communications between two network devices, such as ISP network access servers and VPN gateways. It is transparent to users, but it does not protect communications between users' systems and ISPs.
- **Network layer VPNs** provide secure communication between two hosts or networks without modifying any applications. IPsec is the most common network layer VPN; it is used to secure some or all communications between two endpoints. In addition to protecting the data in the packet, IPsec also protects the IP information, such as IP addresses. IPsec VPNs only support IP and provide less flexibility and control for protecting specific applications.
- So-called **application layer "VPNs"** are protocols that allow encryption to be added to application data. These are not really VPNs because there is no network involved.

Table 6-1. Comparison of SSL and Alternatives

Name	Primary Strengths	Primary Weaknesses	Potential Cases for Use Instead of SSL
PPTP	+ Can protect non-IP protocols	- Requires client software to be configured (and installed on hosts without a built-in client) - Has known security weaknesses - Does not offer strong authentication - Only supports one session per tunnel	None
L2TP	+ Can protect non-IP protocols + Can support multiple sessions per tunnel + Can use authentication protocols such as RADIUS + Can use IPsec to provide encryption and key management services	- Requires client software to be configured (and installed on hosts without a built-in client)	Protecting dial-up communications
L2F	+ Can protect non-IP protocols + Transparent to clients + Can use authentication protocols such as RADIUS	- Requires each ISP's participation - Does not protect communications between the clients and the ISP - Does not offer encryption; must rely on PPP encryption services, which have known weaknesses	None

Name	Primary Strengths	Primary Weaknesses	Potential Cases for Use Instead of SSL
IPsec	+ Already supported by most operating systems + Can provide strong encryption and integrity protection + Transparent to clients in gateway-to-gateway architecture + Can use a variety of authentication protocols	- Can only protect IP-based communications - Requires client software to be configured (and installed on hosts without a built-in client) for host-to-gateway and host-to-host architectures - Does not protect communications between the clients and the IPsec gateway in gateway-to-gateway architectures	Protecting all communications between networks, such as supporting connectivity for a remote site
SSL	+ Already supported by all major Web browsers + Can provide strong encryption and integrity protection + Can provide multiple layers of authentication + Transparent to users + Granular access control	- Can only protect TCP-based communications - Requires application servers and clients to support SSL - Configured on an application-by-application basis	N/A

Table 6-2 lists the TCP and UDP port numbers and IP protocols associated with SSL VPNs and the alternative VPN protocols described in Section 6. This information may be helpful in configuring other network security devices, such as firewalls and routers, to permit VPN activity to pass through.

Table 6-2. IP Protocols and TCP/UDP Port Numbers for VPN Protocols

VPN Protocol	IP Protocols
PPTP	47 (Generic Routing Encapsulation) 6 (TCP), port 1723
L2TP	17 (UDP), port 1701
L2F	17 (UDP), port 1701
IPsec	50 (Authentication Header, for AH connections) 51 (Encapsulating Security Payload, for ESP connections) 17 (UDP), port 500 (for Internet Key Exchange, whether or not NAT-Traversal is used) 17 (UDP), port 4500 (for Internet Key Exchange using NAT-Traversal)
SSL	6 (TCP), port 443

7. Case Study

This section presents an SSL VPN solution planning and implementation case study. The case study begins by describing a real-world security requirement scenario: protecting network communications between remote users and a main office. The case study then discusses possible solutions for the security requirement and explains why an SSL VPN architecture was selected over the alternatives. The next section of the case study discusses the design of the solution and also provides some details of the implementation of the solution prototype, including examples of configuring the solution using commonly available equipment and software.

The case study is not meant to endorse the use of particular products, nor are any products being recommended over other products. A fictional combination of several common products was chosen so that the case study would demonstrate a variety of solutions. **Organizations and individuals should not replicate and deploy the sample entries.** They are intended to illustrate the decisions and actions involved in configuring the solutions, not to be deployed as-is into systems.

The scenario described here is connecting remote users to a single main office. A medium-sized organization has a large population of users that work from remote locations once to several days each week. The organization is research-oriented, and many of these users require access to a broad range of internal IT resources to conduct their research. These resources include email, calendar, file sharing services, and secure shell access on a variety of hosts.

The organization already offers remote access services in the form of a host-to-gateway IPsec solution. This works successfully but has required significant IT labor resources to install and support the client software on user hosts. The current solution also does not provide remote access for hosts based in public locations such as hotels and kiosks. The organization is therefore looking to implement a complementary remote access architecture.

7.1 Identifying Needs and Evaluating Options

The organization specifies its organizational requirements for remote access:

- All users should have access to all internal network resources, especially email and calendar services. This open policy is necessary because of the broad range of IT resources required by users to conduct their research. Users may also be required to authenticate themselves to specific resources such as file shares and databases.

- Users should only have access to a limited set of internal services such as email and calendaring if they are using public hosts (e.g., hosts located in environments such as hotels and Internet cafes).

- A small population of users outside of the organization, human resources (HR) staff from the parent organization, should have access to a limited set of internal HR applications.

After articulating these requirements, the organization considers its options for remote access:

- **Network Layer Solution: IPsec VPN.** As mentioned earlier, the organization has already established IPsec-based network layer VPN services for remote users. Many users are satisfied with this solution, but it can be cumbersome for IT staff to support because each host requires client software to be installed and supported. Moreover, hosts without the preinstalled client software cannot access internal resources.

- **Transport Layer Solution: SSL VPN.** The organization could provide an SSL VPN between the remote users and the office over the Internet. Network extension is the most flexible option because it provides broad access for users into an internal network.

- **Application Layer Solution: Application Modification.** The organization could modify every application required for remote access. Applications such as SSH are already supported for remote access. Due to the broad range of relevant applications, it is not considered feasible to modify all of them.

The organization decides to develop an SSL VPN solution. This solution will complement and not replace the existing IPsec VPN services. It is assumed that some users will stay with the IPsec solution, but others will migrate to SSL VPN over time. The organization purchases a commercial appliance with a support contract to ensure the existence of vendor support.

7.2 Designing the Solution

The organization goes through the process described in Section 4.3 to design the SSL VPN solution. It first designs an access control policy to determine who can access internal resources and under what conditions. The next step is to create an endpoint security policy that enforces access control, usually with host integrity checks. Creating an authentication infrastructure follows, and designing the architecture and deciding on encryption are the last steps.

7.2.1 Access Control Policy

The organization goes through the four major steps to designing an access control policy that are described in Section 4.3.1:

1. **List the resources that will be accessed through the SSL VPN.** Users should have access to all internal network resources, so these resources can all be grouped together. If a specific resource such as a file share or database requires additional authentication, then this takes place when a user accesses the resource. The only exception to this policy of grouping all resources is a set of HR applications that only a small set of external users is authorized to access. Note that these users may not access the other internal resources that other users can access.

2. **List the groups or users.** Most users are in one main group that has network connectivity to all internal resources. A smaller group is composed of external users that have access to the set of HR applications mentioned in the previous step.

3. **List the conditions under which the resources should be accessible by the groups.** There are several conditions for accessing resources:

    - Users must use hosts managed by the organization to gain access to internal resources. These organization-managed hosts all have a system registry key installed that can be checked to verify their identity.

    - Users who login from systems in a public location such as a kiosk or Internet café or use their personal computers can only access a limited set of Web-based applications such as email, calendaring, and employee phone directory.

    - The small group of external users that access the HR applications must also use organization-managed hosts to gain access to these applications.

- All hosts, public or otherwise, must be running the latest version of Windows with critical security updates installed and an antivirus package with an up-to-date virus signature database. They must also have a firewall program installed and running. Any host not meeting these requirements is not permitted to login.

4. **List how the VPN should be used to access the resources.** Resources are accessible in different ways:

    - The organization's internal resources are accessible by network extension because a broad number of them are hosted on multiple servers. Also, some Web-based applications do not function properly when proxying is used, so network extension must be used.

    - When users login from public hosts that are not organization-managed, they can access a set of Web-based applications via proxy.

    - The set of HR applications are accessible by network extension because some require many interlocking programs and cannot be accessed by other means.

Table 7-1 summarizes the organization's access control policy.

Table 7-1. Organization's Access Control Policy

Resource	Group	Condition	Access Type
Internal resources (except HR applications)	Users	Organization-managed host	Network extension
Web applications	Users	Any host running a recent version of Windows with critical updates installed and updated antivirus and firewall software	Proxy
HR applications (only)	HR users	Organization-managed host	Network extension

7.2.2 Endpoint Security Policy

The organization designs an endpoint security policy to enforce access control. The policy is mainly driven by a prelogin sequence executed by the SSL VPN appliance before a user logs in. This sequence runs host integrity checks that require the host to download and run active content controls. These controls or applets ensure that the host complies with the organization's endpoint security policy.

The endpoint security policy is based on the access control policy and elaborates further:

- An organization-managed host is identified by a registry key indicating that the host is managed by the organization. The host integrity check only needs to find this key to verify the host's identity. Organization-managed hosts use network extension to gain full access to the internal network. A packet filter is configured on the SSL VPN to prevent these hosts from accessing the restricted set of HR applications. If a user is permitted to use the restricted set of HR applications, a packet filter is configured on the SSL VPN to prevent the user from accessing any resource outside the HR applications. Users are permitted to keep all cookies, Web browser cache entries, and downloaded files and attachments.

- A host that is not organization-managed or is personally owned can only access Web applications via proxy. The SSL VPN session is established in a virtual storage space and all data stored or downloaded during the session is erased after logout.

- All hosts must run one or more specific versions of Windows, with each specific version using the most current set of updates. Critical security updates are also required to be installed. The host must run an antivirus software program certified by the organization that is active and uses a virus signature database that has been updated in the past month. The host must also run a firewall program.

7.2.3 Authentication Scheme

The organization has an existing RADIUS authentication infrastructure for multiple resources such as databases and email servers. The SSL VPN appliances use the same RADIUS servers to authenticate users as they login to the SSL VPN portal. The groups that are defined by the access control policy are configured in RADIUS. So most users belong to one large RADIUS group, and the external users granted access to the HR applications are put into another smaller RADIUS group.

The SSL VPN appliances determine this group information from RADIUS so they can dynamically map users into the correct group. For example, a user who is a member of the HR Users' RADIUS group is only given access to the HR applications.

Users authenticate themselves via two-factor authentication. Each user must type in a password and use a physical token to enter a one-time password generated by the token. Table 7-2 shows the authentication method for each internal resource.

Table 7-2. Organization's Authentication Methods

Resource	Group	Condition	Authentication
Internal resources (except HR applications)	Users	Organization-managed host	RADIUS (password and token)
Web applications	Users	Any host running a recent version of Windows with critical updates installed and updated antivirus and firewall software	RADIUS (password and token)
HR applications (only)	HR Users	Organization-managed host	RADIUS (password and token)

For server authentication, the organization purchases an SSL server certificate from a CA whose root certificate is already installed in most common browsers and installs the SSL server certificate on the SSL VPN appliance.

7.2.4 Architecture Design

The organization designs an architecture incorporating the SSL VPN appliances within its existing network infrastructure. It performs configuration of the appliances and devises a management policy.

7.2.5 Selection of Hardware Configuration

The organization chooses an appliance solution developed by a commercial vendor. Hardware appliances are the most common type of SSL VPN hardware on the market today, and they possess the advantages of being preconfigured and already hardened by the vendor. Furthermore, support is more straightforward because the device configuration is standardized.

7.2.6 Device Placement and Firewall Configuration

The organization adopts an internal SSL VPN approach for device placement. Access to TCP port 443 on the SSL VPN for all external addresses is added to the corporate firewall; no other access rules are added to the firewall. This is similar to the architecture shown in Figure 4-2.

7.2.7 Routing Policy

The organization prohibits split tunneling, so the remote access host sends all traffic destined for internal subnets and the rest of the Internet through the VPN tunnel. Traffic destined for machines outside the organization's perimeter is blocked by the SSL VPN. In this case, attempts to go off the corporate network directly from the user's system are blocked. Some SSL VPNs include *hairpin proxies* that allow VPN users to leave the network, but only by traversing the SSL VPN gateway which has been set up as a normal outgoing firewall.

The organization has a main headquarters location and several branch offices, but it only deploys SSL VPN appliances at headquarters. All of the organization's internal IT resources are available at headquarters.

7.2.8 High Availability

The organization is pursuing a high availability strategy. The VPN appliance supports high availability with an active/passive architecture. Configuration settings are mirrored across both devices, so any configuration change made to the active device is automatically copied to the passive device's configuration. VPN session information is also mirrored; users do not have to reauthenticate after a device failure, but existing TCP connections are broken and do have to be reestablished.

7.2.9 Management

The management policy for the VPN appliances is consistent with the organization's security policy. Administrative access is only supported on the appliance's internal interface and is limited to a small set of IP addresses. Accounts with limited administrative access are created and assigned to different groups, such as one account that can review system logs and another account that can update the host integrity checks to search for recent security updates.

Configuration settings are backed up each week to a central server. The organization also uses a set of appliances for testing and staging. They are configured identically to the live units, and any updates or patches are applied on them first.

The appliances are monitored by the organization's network management system. The network management system periodically pings the appliances' IP addresses and polls the appliances' SNMP management information base (MIB). It compares data from the MIB with known operational values to search for any potential operational issues.

7.2.10 Client Software Selection

The prelogin sequence requires a remote access host to download and execute active content so the host integrity checks can be performed. The desktop management policies for the organization-managed hosts are configured to permit specific active content controls to run locally.

7.2.11 Portal Design

The organization uses the portal provided by the VPN appliance vendor. It provides some customization such as altering the banner graphics to be consistent with the organization's logo and colors. It also only displays options that the user is authorized to access. For example, if a user is in the group that is only allowed to view the HR Web sites, only those sites are listed on the user's portal page.

7.2.12 Encryption Scheme

The organization requires FIPS 140-2 compliance for its SSL VPN solution. As a result, the organization verifies the level of FIPS compliance of the system before purchasing it. The organization configures the SSL VPN to only permit logins from client browsers that use SSL cipher suites with FIPS-approved cryptography. The appliance is also configured to require browsers to support TLS 1.0 for SSL connections.

7.3 Implementing a Prototype

After the organization designs the SSL VPN solution, it implements and tests a prototype of the design. The prototype is initially configured and tested in a laboratory network and is moved later to a production network so access to actual internal resources can be tested. The laboratory network replicates the addresses of the corporate network, and thus needs to be completely unconnected to the corporate network. The test network includes a firewall with the same configuration as the corporate firewall, and example servers that have the same capabilities and the same addresses as the servers that will be accessed through the SSL VPN.

The organization develops a test plan to evaluate functionality and connectivity. The plan is based on Section 4.3 and includes tests for connectivity, authentication, access control, endpoint security, and client interoperability. Users of multiple operating systems (e.g., Windows, Linux, Macintosh), device types (e.g., laptops, PDAs, smart phones) and Web browsers (e.g., Internet Explorer, Firefox, Mozilla, Safari) must be able to access internal resources from outside the network. If users are using organization-managed hosts, then they should be able to do everything they could do if they were located in their offices. Multiple scenarios such as a user logging in from a public host or a host that has an out of date virus database must be tested. The testers also validate that people with different types of RADIUS credentials only get the expected type of access when they log in during the test.

7.3.1 Example configuration steps

Different SSL VPNs have different administrative interfaces. Many allow control through Web browsers, while some use custom programs, and still others use old-style command line interfaces (CLI). In this section, a fictitious SSL VPN that has a browser interface is described along with examples of steps that might be taken to implement the rules from the scenario.

The interface has four major sections:

- System

- Users
- Access
- Policies.

To begin, the administrator needs to configure the addresses of the Ethernet interface on the SSL VPN. The administrator goes to the *Ethernet* choice in the System menu and sets the address assigned to the SSL VPN on the inside of the corporate network. Because this system is configured inside the existing network, no routing needs to be defined; had this SSL VPN been located outside the firewall or on the DMZ, the administrator would need to specify routing information.

Using the *Add User Group* choice of the Users menu, the administrator creates a group called "NormalUsers". In this dialog box, the administrator specifies which authentication mechanisms are used (a password and a physical token) and specifies how the authentication is validated (using the existing RADIUS server). The administrator specifies that participation in the NormalUsers group for the VPN is given to people whom the RADIUS server labels as "User". They use the Add User Group choice to add a second group, "HROnlyUsers", but participation in that group is the people the RADIUS server labels as "HR Users".

The Access menu allows the administrator to define those resources to which the members of each user group have access. Using the *Add Access Group* command, the administrator creates an access group called "NormalFullAccess" that links "NormalUsers" to all network services, using a network extension program from the SSL VPN. The network extension's packet filter is set up to block TCP ports 80 and 443 of the addresses of the Web servers that are controlled by the HR department. The administrator also selects *only display available resources* for this access group.

Next, for users accessing the SSL VPN from equipment that is not owned by the organization, the administrator uses the *Add Access Group* command to create an access group called "NormalPartialAccess" that links "NormalUsers" only to TCP port 80 of the addresses for the three Web servers that have the corporate calendar, the Web mail system, and the employee phone directory, using a reverse Web proxy, and selects only *display available resources*. Last, the administrator creates the "HRAccess" group that links "HROnlyUsers", using a network extension program from the SSL VPN to allow access to only TCP ports 80 and 443 of the addresses of the Web servers that are controlled by the HR department, and selects *only display available resources*.

The three access lists each have policies associated with them, so the administrator uses the *Policy List* command in the *Policies* menu to create a list of policies. The dialog box starts with an empty list, and the administrator clicks the *Add* button to create the first policy. In that dialog box, the administrator specifies that everyone in the NormalFullAccess group must use the following policies:

- The remote host is managed by the organization.
- The latest version of one or more specific versions of Windows is being used.
- The most current set of patches and security updates has been applied to the operating system.
- An approved antivirus program is running.
- An approved firewall program with an approved configuration is running.
- Split tunneling is not permitted.
- The protocol used must be TLS 1.0 or later.

- The cryptographic protocol being used must be one that complies with FIPS 140-2.

After creating this policy, the administrator creates similar policies for everyone in the NormalPartialAccess and HRAccess groups.

The last steps are to configure the management of the SSL VPN itself. In the *Administrators* command in the System menu, the administrator changes the default password that came with the system and sets the range of IP addresses that can be used to administer the system. In the same dialog box, the administrator also creates additional administrative accounts with limited rights, such as for viewing particular logs. Under the *Backup* command in the System menu, the administrator sets up automatic weekly backups to be sent to an FTP server on the internal network. The *SNMP* command in the System menu is used to allow monitoring of the device.

The *Replication* command in the System menu allows configuration of the high availability feature described earlier. The administrator enters the address of the other server in the high availability group and specifies that this server is the "master" of the group.

7.4 Deploying and Managing the Solution

The organization employs a pilot program to deploy the solution. It solicits volunteers who can contribute their user experience and help to troubleshoot any problems with connectivity or interoperability. The SSL VPN development staff also produces documentation to help in establishing VPN connectivity. The documentation assists users in enabling the host integrity checks to be executed on their hosts, and it addresses frequently asked questions.

7.5 Summary

Section 7 covered a case study for planning and implementing an SSL VPN system for an organization. The steps described in this section follow the recommendations and guidelines given throughout this document for choosing and setting up an SSL VPN. It should be emphasized that the scenario described in this section is for a fictitious organization and that the steps taken by a real organization would likely be different from those given here.

The portrayed organization first identified its needs based on its current operations and its stated future goals for secure remote access. In designing the proposed solution, the organization followed the typical steps of creating both an access control and an endpoint security policy: laying out its methods for authentication of users, designing an overall architecture for the expected remote access solution, selecting the hardware needed to meet its goals, specifying where in its current network the hardware will go, determining whether or not it needs a high availability solution, creating a management policy for the system and users, selecting the client software, designing the portal that the users will see when they connect to the system, and developing an encryption policy.

After this design was completed, the organization implemented a prototype of the system before deploying it fully. The test plan for this prototype involved creating a sample configuration for the network access, the list of users for the system, definitions of the types of access that will be given to the users, and a specific policy plan linking the users to the types of access as well as other policy restrictions on the users.

Appendix A—Glossary

Selected terms used in the *Guide to SSL VPNs* are defined below.

Access Control: The process of permitting or restricting access to applications at a granular level, such as per-user, per-group, and per-resources.

Agent: A host-based IPS program that monitors and analyzes activity and performs preventive actions; OR a program or plug-in that enables an SSL VPN to access non-Web-based applications and services.

Application Layer: Layer of the TCP/IP protocol stack that sends and receives data for particular applications such as DNS, HTTP, and SMTP.

Application Translation: A function that converts information from one protocol to another.

Authentication: The process a VPN uses to limit access to protected services by forcing users to identify themselves.

Availability: The ability for authorized users to access systems as needed.

Confidentiality: The ability to protect data so that unauthorized parties cannot view the data.

Customization: The ability to control the appearance of the SSL VPN Web pages that the users see when they first access the VPN.

Data Link Layer: Layer of the TCP/IP protocol stack that handles communications on the physical network components such as Ethernet.

Diffie-Hellman: A method used to securely exchange or establish secret keys across an insecure network. Ephemeral Diffie-Hellman is used to create temporary or single-use secret keys.

Full Tunneling: A method that causes all network traffic to go through the tunnel to the organization.

Header: A portion of a packet that contains layer-specific information such as addresses.

High Availability: A failover feature to ensure availability during device or component interruptions.

Integrity: The ability to detect even minute changes in the data.

Network Extension: A method of providing partial or complete network access to remote users.

Network Layer: Layer of the TCP/IP protocol stack that is responsible for routing packets across networks.

Payload: Consists of the information passed down from the previous layer.

Portal VPN: A single standard SSL connection to a Web site (the portal) that allows a remote user to securely access multiple network services via a standard Web browser.

Proxy: An intermediary device or program that provides communication and other services between a client and server.

Scalability: The ability to support more users, concurrent sessions, and throughput than a single SSL VPN device can typically handle.

Signature: The ability to trace the origin of the data.

Split Tunneling: A method that routes organization-specific traffic through the SSL VPN tunnel, but routes other traffic through the remote user's default gateway.

Transport Layer: Layer of the TCP/IP protocol stack that is responsible for reliable connection-oriented or connectionless end-to-end communications.

Tunnel VPN: An SSL connection that allows a remote user to securely access a wide variety of protocols and applications, through a tunnel that is running under SSL, via a Web browser, generally augmented by a client application or plug-in..

Virtual Private Network: A virtual network built on top of existing networks that can provide a secure communications mechanism for data and IP information transmitted between networks.

Appendix B—Acronyms

Selected acronyms used in the *Guide to SSL VPNs* are defined below.

AD	Active Directory
AH	Authentication Header
API	Application Programming Interface
ARP	Address Resolution Protocol
CA	Certificate Authority
CEO	Chief Executive Officer
CHAP	Challenge Handshake Authentication Protocol
CIFS	Common Internet File System
CLI	Command Line Interface
CMS	Cryptographic Message Syntax
CMVP	Cryptographic Module Validation Program
CRL	Certificate Revocation List
DES	Data Encryption Standard
DMZ	DeMilitarized Zone
DNS	Domain Name System
DSA	Digital Signature Algorithm
DSS	Digital Signature Standard
ESP	Encapsulating Security Payload
FIPS	Federal Information Processing Standard
FISMA	Federal Information Security Management Act
FTP	File Transfer Protocol
GRE	Generic Routing Encapsulation
HMAC	Keyed-Hash Message Authentication Code
HR	Human Resources
HTTP	HyperText Transfer Protocol
ICMP	Internet Control Message Protocol
IDS	Intrusion Detection System
IETF	Internet Engineering Task Force
IGMP	Internet Group Management Protocol
IKE	Internet Key Exchange
IMAP	Internet Message Access Protocol
IP	Internet Protocol
IPComp	IP Payload Compression Protocol
IPS	Intrusion Prevention System
IPsec	Internet Protocol Security
IPv4	Internet Protocol version 4
IPv6	Internet Protocol version 6
IPX	Internetwork Packet Exchange
ISP	Internet Service Provider
IT	Information Technology

ITL	Information Technology Laboratory
L2F	Layer 2 Forwarding
L2TP	Layer 2 Tunneling Protocol
LAN	Local Area Network
LDAP	Lightweight Directory Access Protocol
MAC	Message Authentication Code
MIB	Management Information Base
MPPE	Microsoft Point to Point Encryption
MS-CHAP	Microsoft Challenge Handshake Authentication Protocol
MTU	Maximum Transmission Unit
NAT	Network Address Translation
NetBEUI	NetBIOS Extended User Interface
NetBIOS	Network Basic Input/Output System
NIST	National Institute of Standards and Technology
OMB	Office of Management and Budget
PAP	Password Authentication Protocol
PC	Personal Computer
PDA	Personal Digital Assistant
PGP	Pretty Good Privacy
PIN	Personal Identification Number
PKI	Public Key Infrastructure
POP	Point of Presence
PPP	Point-to-Point Protocol
PPTP	Point-to-Point Tunneling Protocol
QoS	Quality of Service
RADIUS	Remote Authentication Dial-In User Server
RC4	Rivest Cipher 4
RCP	Remote Copy Protocol
RFC	Request for Comment
RMON	Remote Monitoring
RSA	Rivest Shamir Adleman
S/MIME	Secure MultiPurpose Internet Mail Extensions
SHA	Secure Hashing Algorithm
SLA	Service Level Agreement
SMTP	Simple Mail Transfer Protocol
SNMP	Simple Network Management Protocol
SP	Special Publication
SQL	Structured Query Language
SSH	Secure Shell
SSL	Secure Sockets Layer
TACACS	Terminal Access Controller Access Control System
TCP	Transmission Control Protocol

TCP/IP	Transmission Control Protocol/Internet Protocol
TLS	Transport Layer Security
UDP	User Datagram Protocol
URL	Uniform Resource Locator
USB	Universal Serial Bus
VoIP	Voice over Internet Protocol
VPN	Virtual Private Network